Studymates

The War Poets 1914–18

The secrets of poems from the Great War

Stephen Wade

BA MA PhD

www.**studymates**.co.uk

© 2003 by Stephen Wade

First published in 2003 by Studymates Limited, PO Box 2, Bishops Lydeard, Somerset
TA4 3YE, United Kingdom.

Telephone: (01823) 432002
Fax: (01823) 430097

Typeset by PDQ Typesetting, Newcastle-under-Lyme
Printed and bound by Baskerville Press, Salisbury, Wiltshire

Contents

Preface

POETS OF THE FIRST WORLD WAR

Unusually, the poets of the First World War combine considerable popularity with a high critical reputation. While they have been fortunate in having anthologists and critics as perceptive and committed as Jon Silkin and Samuel Hines to support their cause, it is perhaps the case that the soulscapes as well the landscapes of the trenches exactly coincided with the emergence of literary Modernism to make their work both aesthetically adventurous and yet deeply moving. The appalled, wounded and fractured sensibilities created on the battlefields of northern France found their natural expression in the fragmentary, probably Godless, but still potentially mythopaeic literary and poetic forms of Brooke, Rosenberg, Sassoon, Owen, Edward Thomas and many other poets – to say nothing of the haunted semi-realistic landscapes and battlescapes of painters like Paul Nash and Christopher Nevinson. The outrage, indignation and disillusionment of these artists discovered, in the halting but still ambitious modes of Modernism, a way to make accessible feelings which might have been unimaginable if they had not actually been felt. In the battlefields of the Somme, the Modernist imagination had to some extent been pre-empted and prefigured not as a terrible metaphorical and mythic possibility, but as nothing more than the literal (if incomprehensible) truth.

It is important to remember, too, that much writing produced in direct response to the First World War took time to find a full formal means of expression. Some of the most successful literary works about the First World War are the product of a tortured and extended process of forgetting and recalling in which the fragments of available memory are tested for their authenticity and their artistic potential. From such extended meditations and obsessions came autobiographical reminiscences like Robert Graves's *Goodbye To All That*, Helen Thomas's poignant memoir of her poet-husband Edward Thomas calling out his last goodbyes, increasingly faintly, across the Dorset hills as he left for France and Siegfried Sassoon's various *Memoirs*, at once both elegiac and angry. There were novels of both military recall and failed post-war re-adjustment like 'Private 19022's' *Her Soldiers We* (1930) with its stunning printed black and white Expressionist cloth cover. There were also extended poetic meditations like David Jones's difficult and persistently underrated epic poem *In Parenthesis* (1937). Other writing of the 1930s, like A.G.MacDonell's *England Their England*, published in 1933 but directly built out of the War experience, focusses on constructing an elegy for a rural pre-War England now lost beyond recall. Many influential and accomplished writers remained buried in this mass of material until recent years, and it is good to find this study including poets such as Ivor Gurney, one of the key 'lost' voices of the period. So the War went on being fought in 'the popular memory' (to use Hines's phrase) for many years after 1918, and its meaning still remains open to contest.

Dr Wade's book seeks to represent this combination of urgent emotional compulsion and sustained literary experimentation in First World War poetry to those of you beginning to study this period and its many literary manifestations. The basic task, to translate into language something that had never been conceptualised before, and thus lacked an established vocabulary or literary form, haunted the writers of the time. Edmund Blunden, in the Introductory comments to his 1928 *Undertones of War*, acknowledges his experiences to have been 'very local, limited, incoherent'. Despite making his best literary efforts and spending twelve years brooding on his time as a soldier Blunden can only say of his audience 'Neither will they understand'. This sense of the remoteness, extremity and sheer linguistic *inconceivability* of their War experience is something many of these writers hold in common, yet their outrage, disillusionment and sense of common humanity press them into speech. Dr Wade's book is written as an introduction to just these complex issues. This book is about writing that is both simple in its deeply felt emotional origins and complex in its awareness of the literary problems posed by Modernist writing.

Brian Maidment
Professor of English, University of Salford.

1

Studying the Poetry of War

One-minute summary – In many ways, although the poetry of the soldier poets of the Great War has apparently been thoroughly studied and discussed, readers new to this work will always feel a profound sense of its uniqueness. To understand this poetry, the student has to comprehend the sheer enormity of the suffering and loss of life in a theatre of war that was at once hellish and yet paradoxically a cause of massive social change. The first step is to consider writing about war and conflict in general, then move on to understand the historical context. In passing, we look at the nature of how suffering which is transmuted into art or literature is often part of a process of catharsis – of somehow easing the pain by talking or writing creatively about its nature. In this chapter you will learn:

▶ the preparatory thinking involved
▶ how to comprehend the suffering behind the poetry
▶ how to relate the historical events to the writing
▶ how to form concepts about war writing generally.

The experience of destruction

Entrenched images
There is a huge body of writing about war in English literature, from an Elizabethan *Ballad of Agincourt* to Tennyson's famous poem about the Crimean War, *The Charge of the Light Brigade*, but the poetry written during the first world war (1914–1918) is unique. The poetry written during that period was not all produced in the trenches, but the popular imagination has come to define that war in terms of a miserable, hellish conflict involving extended stalemates in a landscape of mud and bombs.

There is some truth in these media-defined images, but what happens more often is that it becomes a war involving incomprehensible arithmetic. The history books on the subject quote figures such as 20,000 British casualties in the first hour of the battle of the Somme (1916) or that the total British and Commonwealth military casualties for the disaster of Gallipoli (1915) came to 260,000 men.

At the heart of this experience for those involved is a completely unexpected and extended trauma – the volunteers who joined up believed that the war 'would be over by Christmas'. The generals at the beginning still thought of a battle as being cavalry-based, and asked Britain to provide hundreds of thousands of horses. They were utterly wrong.

Attrition and shell-shock

More typical of the battle front was the condition of infantry being penned up in deep trenches and fighting a steady war of attrition (which meant gradually breaking down the opposition by artillery fire and infantry charges at the opposition trenches). It also meant, by 1915, the experience of poison gas and shell-shock for some of the soldiers at the front. The bulk of the poetry comes from this horrendous turmoil and desperate friendships formed within a life on the edge, facing death at any moment.

Destruction in all senses

The pictorial image we have of trench warfare, as in the paintings of Paul Nash or on documentary film, is mainly that of a landscape being destroyed: huge bomb craters, skeletal trees, ruined houses and lines of sandbags and barbed wire. But the writing of the time gives witness to more than land being destroyed. The war involved the destruction of a generation of young men. It also destroyed much of the British confidence that had built a massive empire across the world. Some writers suggest that it even destroyed the innocence of the West in general.

Honour

Certainly a new and very different world emerged after the five years of war. The poets often wrote as if the war was Armageddon

– the Biblical 'final war' that would signal the end of life on earth. Often the poetry is about a vision of new relationships and new beginnings, and about the impossibility of accepting a belief in nothing. At the centre of this is a feeling in the writers that they were destined to die for a noble cause. The keynote was sounded by Rupert Brooke, whose sonnet, *The Dead* has the lines:

> Honour has come back, as a king, to earth,
> And paid his subjects with a royal wage.

The first attitude of mind you need when studying the early phase of the war is an understanding of this concept of 'honour'. Readers need to remember that recent wars in Africa or India had involved the notion of fighting to give faith and proper beliefs to non-Christians. Added to this is the propaganda around at the time that smeared Germany as a militaristic and cruel nation who were out to control Europe and do unspeakably harsh and amoral things to neighbouring countries.

Writing as catharsis

The concept of *catharsis*, which literally means 'cleansing or purifying' goes back to Aristotle in classical Greece, and was originally applied to tragedy. It is an idea that tries to explain that unique sense of release when emotions are unburdened as we are given an outlet to express the pain involved. It is easy to see how this applies to war poetry. In the particular situation of the Western Front, which was largely infantry warfare of a prolonged and traumatic kind, writing in various forms provided this cathartic release. At the horrific battles in Ypres, (known as 'Wipers' by the British) the troops printed a magazine called *Wipers News*. Many men wrote journals and diaries, and of course, some wrote fiction and poetry.

Some aspects of cathartic writing are:

1. A tendency to relive the experience in close detail.

2. A need to set up a narrative viewpoint – to distance the pain.

3. A compulsion to explain something often beyond words.

4. A need to try to make sense of the experience.

Figure 1.1. Aspects of cathartic writing.

Of course, what must be remembered in the case of the Great War is that many of the 'Tommies' were not professional soldiers and were in fact, people who were quite accustomed to writing and creativity in their lives.

Expressing the horror

The cathartic nature of much of the writing discussed in this book may have many guises and the student has to learn to recognise them. For instance, in some poems there sometimes appears to be a delight in detailing the suffering of dying men and in describing the terrors of bomb or gas attacks. Reading the range of different poets and poems, the best strategy is to concentrate on the degrees of personal statements – in other words how **subjective** the poets are. This implies a whole spectrum of possible responses to suffering and consequently a range of ways of expressing the subjects. The poetry of Wilfred Owen is a useful case study here, in that it is possible to read poems he wrote from the front line with totally different levels of closeness to the subjects. For instance in *Dulce Et Decorum Est* he appeals directly to the reader:

If in some smothering dreams you too could pace
Behind the wagon that we flung him in...

In *The Dead-Beat* the third person is used:

> He dropped, – more sullenly than wearily.

In *Futility* Owen is distanced, philosophical:

> Oh what made fatuous sunbeams toil
> To break earth's sleep at all?

The quality of emotion is not strained

Where this leads us in a discussion of what to be aware of in critical writing about cathartic poetry is that as readers, we have to judge the suitability and authenticity of the emotional element in the poem. We will return to this subject in Chapter 2, but meanwhile, consider these aspects of stylistic factors in how we write emotionally and apply them to your reading of the poets:

1. The use or over-use of adverbs ('he sadly, dejectedly walked').

2. Conscious use of conventional poetic diction ('orb' for 'eye').

3. Over-rhetorical language.

4. Involvement of the reader to an extreme degree.

In other words, in many cases, catharsis requires excess in the writing style because it is concerned with excess in the actual subject.

The uniqueness of the Great War

This is an ideal point at which to pause and include a little more essential history. It is often argued that this war was like no other with regard to several things, the writing being just one factor. Certainly, these points support that view: first, it involved cultures well beyond the continent of Europe; second, it affected massive numbers of civilians also, even encompassing a revolution, and finally, it involved the huge participation of non-professional soldiers.

Concerning the latter point, it helps to keep these phases of the war in mind:

Phase 1

The professional soldiers of the BEF (British Expeditionary Force) fought the first confrontations, notably at the first battle of Ypres and casualties were huge. Part of this first phase was the belief still firm in the generals' minds that wars were fought with cavalry. Their recent experience had been in the Boer War in South Africa (1899–1902) and those combats had been largely cavalry-based ones.

Phase 2

Kitchener's Army – and the Battle of the Somme in 1916. After the massive scale of casualties, and the rethinking about the nature of the war by the writers, poets and thinkers, new attitudes emerge.

Phase 3

The entry of the USA into the war in 1917, after continued attacks by German ships on American merchant vessels. Also, stalemate on the Eastern front and the gradual rise of Russia's new army sapped German resources generally.

These phases all contribute to the fact that there had never been a war like this one in human history. The outstanding feature is the prolonged period of deadlock, and the desperate fighting for ground, a little at a time, throughout the five years. Also that this deadlock involved the slaughter of massive numbers of volunteers and conscripts. The toll can be measured by the arrival of conscription, which covered the men up to the age of 41, and that included married men if the rate of enlistment did not reach 50,000 a month.

Unique writing?

Writing critical essays about this poetry demands that you know the place of this poetry in the general culture at the time. The period c.1900–1920 saw a wide burgeoning of poetry openly against the earlier poetry of empire and Victorian values. The anthologies covered the diversity of poems, however, reaching from nature verse to experimental. In this we can see the special quality of poets such as Owen, Sassoon and Rosenberg: they experienced a new vocabulary for poetry. Faced with experiences which were totally new for mankind, they had to find a vocabulary adequate to the task.

Its uniqueness lies perhaps in the startling mix of traditional language and metrical devices and more powerfully direct expression of the diction of trauma. But there is also the rethinking they did about the nature of friendship and relationships within society generally. This last point comes from the startling developments in trench and front line life, in which conditions people had a closeness and special bonds of belonging which inevitably made them compare this with the normal relationships in their home communities.

Understanding poetry and trauma

Before contemplating the poetry of the Great War, it is worthwhile reflecting on the general quality of poetry as something people use and need when in extreme situations. In a secular society, a deep feeling of grief, loss and pressure may express itself in a poem because we reach for a poem instead of a hymn, as people often did, for instance, during the mourning after Princess Diana's death in 1995.

But in 1914, despite the effects of the Industrial Revolution and Darwinism, there were still about a million regular Church of England church-goers, 800,000 Methodists and a million and a quarter Scottish Presbyterians. Also, a large section of the population still worked on the land and knew small village communities.

The life of the trenches, in which death was likely in the near future, changed attitudes; men re-thought the world and its power and class structures. This is most clearly seen, perhaps, in the poetry of Siegfried Sassoon.

The essential historical background

What about the larger questions regarding this remarkable conflict? It helps to bear in mind that the situation was marked by paradoxes: for instance, that the Tsar of Russia, King George V and Kaiser Wilhelm II were cousins. Yet, there had been various alliances in the ten years preceding the war which over-rode these facts and forced nations into war. These events were mainly:

1. The Entente Cordiale of 1904 which was an agreement between England and France standing against the imminent threat of Germany, which was expanding and becoming territorially aggressive ever since the unification of the German states in 1870.

2. The assertion by Britain that Belgian neutrality, in the event of war, should be defended.

3. The expectation of a war with Germany, indicated by such things as the Agadir Crisis of 1911, in which French and German interests in Morocco led to the possibility of a general war(North Africa being a potential naval base for Atlantic activity).

4. The War Book – a systematic record of preparations (notably naval expenditure) produced in Britain since the beginning of the century.

Figure 1.2. Key dates pre-1914.

The familiarity of war

It also needs to be said that war was a familiar activity for Britain, particularly within its empire. Britain had constant warfare to contain and manage throughout most of the nineteenth century, mostly famously the Crimean War (1853–6) The Zulu War (1879–80) and the Boer War (1899–1902). This meant that life in Britain involved a considerable familiarity with the military life;

soldiers would be a common sight in cities, and most middle class families would have sons who were officers.

Grasping the military ethos of 1914

Much of the literature at school and for teenage reading in the Victorian and Edwardian period had been concerned with stressing the male codes of heroism in war. A famous example of this is Sir Henry Newbolt's poem, *Vitaï Lampada* ('the torch of life') in which he compares the school ethos to that of the battlefield:

> The Gatling's jammed and the Colonel dead,
>   And the regiment blind with dust and smoke.
> The river of death has brimmed his banks,
>   And England's far, and Honour a name,
> But the voice of a schoolboy rallies the ranks:
>   Play up! Play up! And play the game!

Unbelievably, this notion of manliness and heroism in war persisted even into the years of the Great War. Magazines like *The Boy's Own* and the novels of Percy F. Westerman are examples of this. The results of this are evident in the statements made by the 1914 generation, as they give the opinion that somehow destiny has meant them to prove themselves in war. Roland Leighton wrote to Vera Brittain in 1914: 'I feel that I am meant to take an active part in this War ... something, if often horrible, yet very ennobling...' (*Testament of Youth*, p. 105).

These attitudes were to provide a profound ironical perspective on the harsh reality of battle in the works of the poets.

Tutorial

Progress questions

1. What were the attitudes to war in literature previous to 1914?

2. List some of the reasons why poetry and catharsis are closely linked together.

3. In what way was the Great War unique?

4. How did the generation of 1914 view the coming of war with Germany?

Discussion points

In each discussion point, you will find an extract from a poem to illustrate the dominant themes of First World War poetry. This one is a section from Laurence Binyon's *For the Fallen*:

> Solemn the drums thrill: Death august and royal
> Sings sorrow up into immortal spheres.
> There is music in the midst of desolation
> And a glory that shines upon our tears.

1. How does the thought of this relate to the kind of ideals the war had?

2. Does it seem to be written by a combatant? If not, why not?

Practical assignments

1. Find images of recruiting posters, boys' comics or similar pictures of soldiery at the time. Find links between these and the thinking in Rupert Brooke's sonnets of 1914.

2. Access a web site (see Reference section) with information about particular battles such as Ypres, Somme or Loos. Compare the factual basis with a poem written in that battle.

3. Survey the poems written in 1914, before the first heavy defeats, and note, list and summarise in your course notes the number of abstract words in the poems. (words such as 'honour', 'duty', wisdom'. 'glory' and so on.

2

Witness and Response

One-minute summary – There are established responses by writers to the experience of war, and understanding these responses means thinking about the actual subjects and treatments of themes by poets. After the broad theoretical and historical material of the opening chapter, this chapter will now be a closer focus on the norms and boundaries of the aspects of war which tend to be in the work of the 1914–18 generation of poets. In this chapter you will learn:

▶ what the traditions and conventions of war poetry are
▶ what issues are involved in the notion of empathy
▶ how poets break with convention in their use of language.

The conventions of war writing

A survey of the literature of war shows that there have always been a whole spectrum of responses, but with the common ground of idealistic patriotism at one extreme and bitter, critical satire at the other. A knowledge of the varying attitudes to the experience of conflict and suffering in battle is essential to an understanding of the poets included here. This chapter deals with the main established attitudes and conventions in a way which will help your essay-writing when you focus on an individual poet.

Patriotism

Clearly, many writers in a war will be there because they see the just cause in their country's participation. Usually, wars involve a defence against an aggressor, of course, but in the case of the Great War, there is no doubt that Germany had crossed frontiers and invaded other countries. British forces had crossed the Channel and were there ostensibly to help the weaker nations against the mightier. But this complicates the 'Englishness' and patriotism in the poetry.

In cases where the soldiers are clearly defending their land against invasion, the subject of the homeland and the need to save a heritage and a culture are obviously central to the writing. In English history, there had not been such an instance since Harold confronted William's Norman forces at Hastings in 1066. Since then, invasions had been factional, as in the Yorkist wars. But in 1914 there had been massive conscription and the propaganda machine has depicted Germany as a ruthless, amoral threat to 'civilisation'.

Poets in the trenches of the Somme did indeed have literary forebears in terms of soldier poets, but there had been very little that could compare with their situation. Yet, whatever one thinks of the beliefs about fighting for England at this time, the fact remains that several poets made the love of England a central feature in their work. We will return to this later in Chapter 4, but for now, note these kinds of writing about England and the sense of Englishness felt by the poets of 1914:

(a) 'Home' contrasted with a foreign, alien environment.

(b) 'Home' as a place representing a civilised world, in contrast to the hellish barbarism of the war.

(c) England as an idyllic, idealised place, in which values of gentlemanly and decent behaviour were important.

(d) England as a haven of nature and the free natural world, untouched by turmoil.

Heroism

Of course, war has always created heroes. Stories and myths abound in the particular context of the Great War. For instance, a Canadian officer, L. Wearmouth, was awarded a posthumous V.C. for extraordinary courage. He actually caught a German grenade and threw it back; later he died while (when wounded) leading an attack against machine guns. One of the most successful poets of the trenches, Siegfried Sassoon (see Chapter 6) was awarded the Military Cross for bravery in the face of fire.

It is not surprising then, that the poetry dealt with heroism as a theme. For Wilfred Owen the heroism was often in the sheer endurance and courage of keeping sane with the horrors of death and pain all around. For others it was the charge and the assault on the enemy. The poems in the anthologies like the one probably used on your course offer the whole range of attitudes. But the tradition of heroism in war is a long one, and there are many famous poems on the subject. A typical one is *A Ballad of Agincourt* by Michael Drayton, written in 1606. This recalls a much earlier British presence on the fields of France, and is openly praiseworthy of Henry V and his army, with such lines as, 'Oh when shall English men/With such acts fill a pen,/Or England breed again/ Such a king Harry!'

Satire

Equally, war invites criticism and writers question the reasons for the war and, of course, the human cost. This also has a long tradition, but it is an interesting exercise to survey the well-known stories in popular culture of war and heroism, such as the films *Zulu* and *The Charge of the Light Brigade*, and to find popular opinion as to what constituted heroism and what is or is not 'noble'. In the Great War, satire emerged more openly after the massive disenchantment of the Somme battles (1916) and the tide turned against patriotism as a subject after such large-scale slaughter. It is interesting that satire against war, in historical perspective here, has often been a popular rather than an elitist standpoint, written by dissenters and critics. What is particularly interesting in the 1916–18 years is that the reader actually follows the process of change and opposition to the war in the work of particular poets.

Witness

Being a witness is also crucial to our understanding of war writing. Think about the relation of a poet to his or her subject. There is a distinction between the poet who actively searches for a subject and the poet who only writes in response to 'inspiration' or some provocation to write. In the case of a war, the subject is constantly there – a huge subject claiming the poet's total attention. Every day in trench warfare a poet will witness something that is potentially a subject for a poem, whether it is boredom or a long, painful dying. Owen said openly that his subject was 'war and the pity of war' but others took more interest in what was in their imagination, and turned from being a writing witness, with a purposeful crusade to tell it 'like it is'.

Objectivity and empathy

Objectivity and empathy are fundamental to the study of war poetry, as a poet's response can vary between a personal, human subjectivity – giving an account of the emotive response – to the effort of actually trying to be in the other person's condition. This latter point is very important. Consider empathy first of all in the literal sense of 'feeling with', that is, a sense of feeling the condition of another person, particularly under stress or pressure. This is hard for any artist, as when Shakespeare writes the character of Juliet (a 14-year-old girl in Renaissance Italy). In war, there is clearly a demand for the poet to respond to horror and the extremes of suffering with both expressions: that of the journalist simply writing down what is observed, coldly, and that of the human being feeling the pain of the other.

The descriptive basis of poetry

Naturally, writing about poetry involves noting the simple level of description in the text. Not all poetic language is about extremes and images; much good writing just notes the physical environment. In a military confrontation, there is a huge amount of activity to convey to the reader. Be aware in your reading and critical writing of the effects of description. In Owen's *Dulce Et Decorum Est* for instance, the opening is purely an account of how the situation looks:

> Bent double, like old beggars under sacks,
> Knock-kneed, coughing like hags, we cursed through sludge.

Notice how every word adds to the overall effect of giving the reader the precise feel and sound of the men and the movement in that grim trench. Starting with a list of the features composing the scene allows Owen to establish a mood and a pace for the poem. Description can include metaphors, of course, but essentially the objective stance is maintained.

The problem of distance

Does poetry in its objective mode do more than provide a more wordy journalism or reportage? Here, we need to consider the nature of a poem as an assemblage of words in a rhythm or rhyme-scheme. With this in mind, it is easy to see how a war poem can create a sound-picture even when the poet remains objective and does not let his emotions invade the people before him. A factor in the impact of war poetry now, in the 21st century, is our image-led society, in which films and videos of war and battle abound; in fact we have so many reproductions and media forms involving battle that we may find it hard to be impressed by a poem which simply describes.

Restraint

We will now consider the idea of restraint and selection of materials: a poet's outstanding method of making his emotive words hit home in the reader. In a poem, we have a minimal form dealing with the maximum power of feeling. The 1914–18 poets were confronted with abominations, and they had circumstances never before experienced around them. In the best poems, these are given to us with a sense of material being selected rather than given all together. The effect is more potent as a result. In a modern action film, for instance, a long battle sequence can have an 'unreal' quality as we treat it as simply a fiction. But when we read an account of such things by an ordinary person who was a witness, the effect can be stunning.

A poet writing with a sense of restraint will also be aware of how much a cliché or a stereotype will be counterproductive in giving a convincing representation of a subject so far from most people's knowledge. For instance, an expected view of a war would conform to that presented in the media 'back home' and such a bland piece of writing will rarely emerge from a restrained angle, rather than the rhetorical fervour of over-statement.

Empathy

In Owen's poem, *Dulce Et Decorum Est* referred to above, the climax of the poem attempts to give us the agony of a young man dying in a gas attack. Owen does this so vividly that he has to use astonishing, sensuous metaphors in order to try to convey the actual suffering: he addresses the reader, openly appealing to our sense of empathy:

> If you could hear, at every jolt, the blood
> Come gargling from the froth-corrupted lungs,
> Obscene as cancer, bitter as the cud
> Of vile, incurable sores on innocent tongues,–

Notice how he has to describe to an extreme – so much so that he searches for similes to give the extremity of the pain being felt.

In other words, writing with empathy is far more extreme an effort than mere sympathy, which may be more distant and vague. Empathy implies that the writer is attempting *to be the other*. The implications of this are staggering, if we note just how language, even in the most skilful hands, can only grope towards the truth, the actuality of the other's condition. But in war poetry we have a useful case study of this tendency in literature, and in your reading you need always to be aware of how this effort is made.

Meditation and reflection

War poetry is one of the most extreme varieties of poetic expression. It asks the poet to express an experience which is 'beyond words' in a sense, and which relates to wider, more philosophical and religious issues. In the poetry of the trenches, the reader can note the element of mental or imaginative effort to transcend the actual stuff of life around the poet and explore the deeper themes. The idea of meditation has a long history in English poetry, often suggesting a speculative thinking based on something in sight, lying before the poet as he takes his thought higher and further. In Owen's work, this is notable, as he was a poet who had earlier in life been brought up as an Evangelical (having a firm Christian faith and a belief in good works) so his meditation poems tap into this inheritance, as in *Futility*, a short poem which illustrates this mode, particularly in its contrast of a set of thoughts on a corpse, a specific physical subject, with the second stanza which goes into a broader meditation:

> Are limbs, so dear achieved, are sides
> Full-nerved, still warm, too hard to stir?
> Was it for this the clay grew tall?

Observe how the speculations and questions are rhetorical – they demand no answer, and their strength is in that fact. This meditational tone and voice in the Great War poetry is one worth special notice, as it leads the reader into considering the ideology of the period and its relation to traditional Christian belief in Western society.

Reflection and the self

This is a good point at which to mention something central to our understanding of this particular conflict: the idea of the self, the individual. Recall here the tendency of war – particularly the infantry-centred war referred to here – to obliterate the sense of the combatant as an individual. His selfhood is taken away as he becomes an anonymous private in the line, with a number next to his name. In many ways, he ceases to have the full identity of the person he was in civilian life. In the context of the trench warfare on the Western Front, this is acutely the case. The poets' reflections were often directed towards this need to be reminded that the unknown soldier was indeed a person with a former life. Owen's work even shows, at times, the nature of the men being eroded to such a degree that they were actually in the landscape: 'Or whether yet his thin and sodden head/Confuses more and more with the low mould' (*Asleep*).

The reflective poem often concerns this expression of self, given with a melancholy, lyrical tone, interior-based, and related to the disappearing sense of self experienced by the soldier on active duty. In reading, be aware of this and how references to the individual are put into texts at odds with the ruling ideology of war.

The experience of shock

At the base of war poetry, there is bound to be the problem of how the almost indefinable trauma in mind and body is to be accounted for. The old issue of how to find words for the experience of pain 'beyond words' is more relevant in the extremes of war literature than in many other contexts. Wilfred Owen is an excellent example of the poet who expresses such acute experience with a variety of styles and vocabularies. When reading his poems concerning such trauma, be careful to list and group the diction according to how it expresses the subject. For instance, in *Dulce Et Decorum Est* he has to describe the horrible sight of the young man in front of him who did not fit his gas mask in time to save himself from the noxious effects. He starts with an overt reference to the impact on his interior imagination:

> In all my dreams, before my helpless sight,
> He plunges at me, guttering, choking, drowning.

It is worth noting that Owen was drafting this at Craiglockhart hospital in October, 1917. That is, as with so many poems, he was rewriting at a distance from the impact of the trauma.

Owen is trying to convey something by means of finding a way to understate his own inner pain while at the same time giving us vivid and expressive verbs to express the soldier's suffering.

Understanding metaphors of war

This is a good point to introduce the nature of established metaphors in war poetry. There is a strong tradition of writing with *hyperbole*: exaggerated expression in order to produce a rhetorical effect. With extreme experience as a subject, it is not surprising that poets in war tend to write with an eye to great polarities of human involvement, whether it is the sheer boredom of awaiting an attack or actually facing the enemy with 'cold steel'. In Julian Grenfell's *Into Battle*, written in the early phase of the war, we have an example:

When approached a poem of this variety it is useful to have a checklist of questions in terms of how trauma is written about:

(a) How explicit is the language used?

(b) Does the poet use an abundance of adjectives?

(c) What senses are appealed to in the process of writing?

(c) Are the words predominantly abstract or tactile/visual?

Figure 2.1. Checklist of questions.

The thundering line of battle stands,
And in the air Death moans and sings;
But Day shall clasp him with strong hands,
And Night shall fold him in soft wings.

This has several features associated with the effects of hyperbole, as in the second line in which Death is *personified*, that is, made to seem to be a human entity (note the capital letter). In fact, personification is used three times here, as 'Day' and 'Night' are equally made into beings of some kind. We need to ask why these stylistic tricks are used in such a context. One answer is that Grenfell is applying poetic, artificial diction which had been used in war poetry since the time of Drayton and before. Implicit here is the assumption that the confrontation is ennobling in some way.

Realism again: a chance to analyse diction
This brings us back to the point about realism discussed in Chapter 1. The issue is often resolved by looking at the poetic diction: the language selected for use in the poem. A general scale of meanings to note is to imagine a range of emotional levels in the language on this spectrum:

1. Mere exact description...10. Simple metaphor...20 conceit

Examples might be:

1. Description:

> A hundred feet he nosedives, then .
> He rights himself and scuds down sky
> Towards the German line again
>> (Edmund Blunden, *Clear Weather*)

2. Simple metaphor:

> Sharp-fanged searches the frost, and shackles the
> sleeping water...
>> (Edmund Blunden, *January Full Moon, Ypres*)

3. Conceit:

> Their eyes are rid
> Of the hurt of the colour of blood for ever,
> Their hearts remain small-drawn
>> (Wilfred Owen, *Insensibility*)

The simple metaphor gives a clear, immediate sensuous or visual impression of the feeling or thought, whereas the conceit asks us to follow unions of more elaborate, less logically constructed images. A famous definition of a conceit was given by Samuel Johnson in the eighteenth century when he said, 'Heterogeneous ideas are yoked by violence together.'

Measuring effects of realism

From the above discussion, it may be seen that there is no yardstick which calculates a conceit as opposed to a metaphor at a simple level. The only guide is the complexity of the diction, and the question arises: does a more complex language suggest a more effectively realistic poem? Not necessarily. Realism can be evoked by the simplest of words, so what you look for is:

(a) The extent to which the poet seems to strain for effects.

(b) The necessity of explanatory notes – written by scholars and editors in your edition.

(c) The relation of the images to an overall directing principle which structures the whole poem.

Tutorial

Practice questions

1. What themes dominated traditional war poetry?

2. Define the term 'empathy' and give examples from Owen's work.

3. Explain how objectivity in a poem is achieved.

4. In this extract from Thomas Hardy's *Drummer Hodge* (written during the Boer War) what aspects of traditional war poetry do you find?

> Young Hodge the Drummer never knew–
> Fresh from his Wessex home–
> The meaning of the broad Karoo*.
> The Bush, the dusty loam,
> And why uprose to nightly view
> Strange stars amid the gloam.

> *karoo – a high plateau

Points for discussion

1. In what ways does the actual material of the 1914–18 poets differ from, say, poets of the Napoleonic or Zulu wars?

2. What are the difficulties which become apparent when a critic tries to establish the success or failure of empathic writing?

Practical assignments

1. Contrast two poems which make reference to England and make notes on the different ways in which they invoke or describe the image of 'home' in their imaginations.

2. Study some drawings and painting from the Great War, such as the work of Stanley Spencer, John Singer Sargent and Paul Nash, or music such as Benjamin Britten's *War Requiem*, and

consider how their representation of extreme suffering compares with the verbal art of Owen and Sassoon. A useful tool here is a book which uses both images and text, such as Robert Giddings' *The War Poets* (Bloomsbury, 1988).

Study Tips

1. Find accounts of the war in the trenches written by ordinary soldiers in letters and diaries. Compare their language with the language of the poets, taking particular note of such things as military slang, nicknames and images. Research the use of these varieties of non-Standard English in the poems.

2. Find a poem written by a poet at home, not involved in the war, and notice how he or she invokes what they have not directly experienced. You might use a text by a more recent poet, such as *Six Young Men* by Ted Hughes, who was born well after the Great War, in 1930, but meditates on a photograph of soldiers from that conflict.

3

How to Read a War Poem

One-minute summary – All poems have certain general qualities of technique in common, but the diversity of subjects means that readers have to approach these texts with an awareness of the features and conventions of this particular variety of poem – or *genre* to use the established term. Examiners will be noting your awareness of the common qualities of poems concerned with war. They will also be aware of your knowledge of what the norm of the poetry of the Great War tends to be. An essay will have to show that you understand the norm, the middle ground, of the typical war poem. Only with that knowledge will you be able to write well on the specific qualities of the poem you discuss in your essay. This chapter is also concerned with the general knowledge required to explain how a short poem works – what its structure is. In this chapter you will learn:

▶ the basic shape and development of a short poem
▶ the issue of the poet's personal vision
▶ how oppositions are used to add interest and power to a poem
▶ how a use of contextual knowledge adds depth to an essay.

The tradition of the lyric 'I'

When we read a poem written in the first person, that is, using the first person pronoun, 'I', in order to narrate the story or feeling of the poem, we experience an interesting set of questions about how poetry appeals to us as individuals. For instance, a poem such as Brooke's *The Soldier* begins with 'If I should die, think only this of me:...' This uses reference to the first person with 'I' and again with 'me'. Simple though this seems, there are various possibilities as to whom the pronoun refers:

1. The poet – in this case, Brooke.

2. The imagined soldier of the poem who contemplates death.

3. The universal extension of the 'I' to mean anyone.

This may seem like splitting hairs, but it is important in many poems when we wish to refer, for instance, to the known facts of the poet's life. In reading Sassoon, for instance, we have the evidence of his *War Diaries* in which he writes a prose account of events and then provides the first draft of a poem based on that experience.

Reading first person

For these reasons, read with care when a poem uses the lyric 'I' and never assume that it refers to the poet himself. As D. H. Lawrence once said, 'Trust the tale, not the teller.' If the poet is clearly 'in the poem' – that is, we have evidence that it is based on biographical data – then we can proceed. A good example is Sassoon's poem, *The Kiss* which is based on his experience of hearing a lecture on using the bayonet from a Major Campbell, (written on 25 April, 1916) and when we read these lines:

> To these I turn, in these I trust –
> Brother Lead and Sister Steel.
> To his blind power I make appeal,
> I guard her beauty clean from rust

We know the circumstances, and we know that the 'I' could refer to (a) Sassoon himself (b) the Major (used ironically) or (c) any private of infantry talking to himself about his bayonet.

The use of the lyric 'I' is therefore a subtle device, useful for writing irony, sarcasm and satire.

The poet in the poem

Here is a summary of the factors involved in using biographical reference in an essay on a poem:

Data from secondary studies – material from a biography such as Jon Stallworthy's book on Wilfred Owen – may provide a reading of a poem.

Data from personal diaries, journals and letters – there is a massive amount of personal writing available which supports the texts of poems.

Data from historical research – as, for instance, when poems are undated, but refer to specific military actions and events.

Data from textual study – some of Owen's undated poems have been dated by study of the watermarks on the paper he used.

Figure 3.1. Using documents as references for study.

Naturally, in the poetry embedded in such a well-documented conflict as the First World War, there is no difficulty in accessing historical data which exists around the personal 'world' of the poem, but it is helpful when preparing an essay to summarise all the factors which play a part in this small world – microcosm – of a particular poem. A good example of this is a poem such as Sassoon's *A Subaltern*, written after the death of one of his closest friends, D. C. Thomas. This has these main constituents:

(a) personal grief and loss

(b) reflection on the past

(c) intense description of the miseries of life in the trenches

(d) Sassoon's relation to him.

In this case, the poet in the poem presents no problem to the critic, and it is acceptable to use the biographical reference in the essay. What is particularly interesting is that the poem touches on one of the pervasive themes of the poetry of this war: friendship and comradeship in hellish conditions.

Working with poems and supporting data

In writing essays on war poetry, it is a positive step to read and relate secondary information to the poems you study, and good advice is to gather a checklist about the poems you select to study in detail, so that in an examination or coursework writing, the secondary information may be introduced. An example would be Owen's poem, *Dulce Et Decorum Est,* which is centrally concerned with a gas attack, so your essay could use these elements:

Context – an awareness of the historical facts: gas was first used on 22 April, 1915, by the Germans at Langemarck. Horrific suffering was caused, hence the phrase 'froth-corrupted lungs' in Owen's poem. Mustard gas filled the lungs with fluid and a greenish substance was coughed up by the victim.

Biography – Owen experienced this first-hand.

Intertextual – relating this poem to others: Owen's poem quotes a Latin phrase about a very different kind of sacrifice for one's nation.

Figure 3.2. Using secondary sources.

Structure and development

This is an ideal point at which to introduce the study of the structure and development of a short narrative or lyric poem. First, be clear about these terms:

> *lyric* – generally concerned with a short reflection or meditation on the subject
>
> *narrative* – having a story element, a sequence of events.

Many of the poems of this war are short narrative, obviously because the poets had urgent and compelling accounts of actions and events to recall for us. But whether lyric or narrative, a short poem tends to have the following basic structure and development:

Stage 1
An establishment of the essential situation: perhaps a person, a location or a specific feeling. It may simply be descriptive.

Stage 2
A development through description or narrative, leading to

Stage 3
A crisis or turning point of some powerful or significant kind.

Stage 4
Finally, a resolution, either with shock, surprise, affirmation, or irony.

In writing your essay, make sure that you comment on how these aspects of development and structure are achieved. Generally, you will be looking for these elements of a poem as you read and make notes:

1. What language devices are used to integrate the different parts of the poem?

2. Do devices such as images or repetitions serve to unify the tone or subject?

3. Does the poem move from an initial position with regard to the subject, finally to a radically different position by the closure?

A model for studying structure and development
A poem that illustrates these techniques very clearly is Owen's *Futility*.

Form the habit of reading poems three times before you write notes on structure. Follow these guidelines:

▶ *Read for form*: *Futility* is a sonnet: it has 14 lines with a rhyme scheme of ABABCCC/ DEDEFFF. In case this is new to you, here is further explanation. The letters refer to the end-rhymes ('sun' and 'sown' end lines 1 and 3). We

start to give letters for each line, so the words rhyming at the ends of lines form a pattern and we can see this at a glance when we see the list of letters. In this way, the 14 lines give this form:
Lines 1–4 alternate end-rhyme
Lines 5–7 all rhymes match – called a triolet or triplet
Lines 8–11 as 1–4
Lines 12–14 as lines 5–7.

▶ *Read for subject and thinking*: The poem begins with a view of a young man who has died, being moved into the sun. So it is simply descriptive. Then, the focus switches from the corpse to the sun, and the reader is addressed with the word 'think'. Grammatically, this is a vocative – it calls to or addresses the reader. So thinking has developed. Finally, lines 11 to 14 are a string of questions about the nature of life, and why there was such a thing as the beginning of life when it led to such unnecessary slaughter.

Now you can write notes on each of these sections.

The three phases discussed
We now return to the three phases of a poem's structure and development above. These might be your notes on *Futility*:

1. *Devices of language that integrate*: the rhyme scheme does this. The reader is closely involved with the tone of the speaker, as the statements are couched in rhyme. Also, Owen's favourite method of giving half- or pararhymes is used here. A pararhyme is a rhyme in which the vowels used may differ slightly, but the sounds around the vowels are the same, so 'seeds' and 'sides' is an example. Consider what effect this has.

2. *Images or repetitions*: notice how the link between the sun and life sustain an idea right through the poem. At the opening, it acts 'gently' and by the closure, the beams are 'fatuous'. He has moved from a specific instance (the death) to a general truth (evolution and the beginnings of all life).

3. *Change of position/tone/viewpoint*: this poem has gone from description of a death, to a dreamy, romantic view of the sun as life-giver, and finally to the sun of science, of time and evolution. Thus the poem begins with a small event and moves to one of the utmost significance.

Looking for oppositions in the text

A poem is a condensed, minimal way of expressing quite complex and profound thought, so therefore it comes as no surprise to learn that a poet will consciously use oppositions to give the thought or feeling a maximum impact. Given that most of these poems have a story to tell, then clearly, as with all stories, there needs to be some force working against another force in the fabric of the poem. Most successful stories work by oppositions such as:

► conflict
► order-disorder
► emotional/reason-based
► small world – larger world

and so on. In *Futility,* as we just discussed, the opposition is concerned with the specific death of the young soldier and the mind-boggling concept of time and human history. As you read the war poems, make a note of any of these oppositions, and acquire the habit of watching for those that recur across several poems by different writers.

Some oppositions are easy to see, and the structure of the poem is notably based on strong contrast. A plain example of this is Owen's poem, *The Send-off.* The poem starts with the young men marching away to war and they '...sang their way/To the siding shed' and went '...secretly like wrongs hushed-up...'. Then, the poem ends with the thought that a few 'may walk back, silent, to their still village wells,/Up half-known roads.'

Contrasts
Note how in this poem the series of contrasts indicated by the language (the poetic *diction*) signals sharp ironies to the reader, as in oppositions in the adjectives:

Opening ten lines – darkening/white/dull/casual/unmoved

The effect is one of the event being mundane and perfunctory, as if it is no longer a public, glorious event, as it was at the beginning of the war.

Closure – (adjectives again) – great/wild/silent/half-known.

Thus the use of contrast is subtle, as even at the ending, when it should be one main idea, there is an irony built in, when the words 'great' and 'half-known' knock against each other uneasily and illogically.

Note-taking and summarising

Drawing all these techniques together, it is useful to think in terms of preparing for writing an essay as a process of assembling a list of ideas which all fit together as you plan the structure of your essay. For example, taking notes involves these skills:

What topics should an essay on a poem or poems cover? Notebook topics should be:

▶ The shaping of the thought and feeling of the poem – the development from the opening to the resolution at the closure.

▶ The patterns of language used, such as images and rhyme.

▶ How the technique relates to the central subject of the poem.

▶ Biographical or background information essential to reading the poem fully.

Figure 3.3. Suggested topics for an essay.

Get into the habit of reading the poems of a poet in chronological order or by theme/subject. Then have a list of the main events and turning-points of the Great War by your side as you read. The habit of relating these two things will ensure that your thinking about the texts becomes comprehensive, although it is still true to say that your emphasis should always be on the poem itself, with the background and contextual notes kept to a minimum.

Patterns of meaning

A good critic of poetry brings together all the factors influencing the poem as an expression of a thought or feeling, and in the case of the poetry of the Great War, the poem and its surrounding references might look something like this:

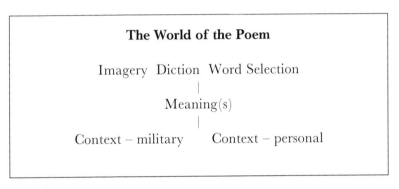

The World of the Poem

Imagery Diction Word Selection

|

Meaning(s)

|

Context – military   Context – personal

Figure 3.4. Factors influencing poem interpretation.

In this way, there is an interplay between the technique and the context. For instance, look at how the word selection (such as army slang) relates to our reading of the context of men in a war setting.

Beware of intention

The other important area is to note that an author's intention is always difficult, if not impossible to be sure of; we have to make an educated guess based on the evidence of the technique and reference. For example, the case of irony illustrates this. We can only assume some irony if either there is a clearly ironic intonation such as 'He did for them all with his plan of attack' or a double meaning such as Sassoon's *In The Pink*, in which he takes the bright, happy meaning of 'in the pink' – doing very well – and then twists it into an ironical message with the lines:

> Tonight he's in the pink, but soon he'll die.
> And still the war goes on – *he* don't know why.

Tutorial

Progress questions

1. In what instance could we be more certain of the use of 'I' in a poem?

2. What considerations arise in deciding what background historical information to use in an essay?

3. List three types of opposition used in the structure of a poem.

4. How is this image ironical? (from Sassoon's poem, *Died of Wounds*)
    I fell asleep ... Next morning he was dead;
    And some Slight Wound lay smiling on the bed.

Points for discussion

1. What problems might arise in assuming a poet writes poems because of statements made in personal diaries?

2. How might a study of battlefield maps help in reading a war poem?

Practical assignments

1. Read Owen's *The Send-off* closely and try to write a prose summary of its story.

2. Write a list of contrasting features and words in any of Owen's poems set in trench life.

3. Compare any of Sassoon's diary notes with the poems arising from the experience. How has the original experience been developed into poetic form?

4

Language and Style

One-minute summary – The next logical step after considering some of the broader historical and literary matters is to focus on the nature of the language and style used most commonly by the majority of the poets of the Great War. This gives the critic a chance to absorb and understand the patterns of thought which tend to be repeated across a variety of poems and poets. Certain uses of language recur, and a set of metaphorical and symbolic references also appear in several poems. Always remember that in a sound, well argued essay you need to show an awareness of the general thinking behind poetry at the time as well as a knowledge of how to analyse a particular poem. For instance, imagery of nature and the countryside is used in a variety of ways by the war poets – sometimes descriptively but sometimes ironically. In this chapter you will learn:

▶ how to read the patterns of imagery in a poem
▶ how imagery works generally in poetry
▶ how word selection determines the central argument and feeling in a poem
▶ how the war poets tried to achieve a new sense of realism.

Contrasting past and present

Naturally, a writer in a war will reflect on his or her past life and make comparisons with the present suffering. This is a simple observation, but it leads to the profound link between poetry and memory. In preparing to write essays on poetry, it pays to reflect on what ways the poets of the Great War generation used the past. How did they use memory creatively and how did it help them write about the present time? A positive first step is to list exactly how memory and poetry are related creatively:

43

> ▶ The past is always being revised and revisited by creative writers.
> ▶ Memory and past time is a resource for generating imagery.
> ▶ The past is in itself an immediate comparison – a tool for contrastive writing.
> ▶ Poetry and memory both share a strong organising principle of emotion.
> ▶ Memory is selective, as poetry is too.

Figure 4.1. How memory and poetry are related creatively.

The past as a determining image in the poetry

Often, poetry written in war has to recreate the past in order to show the radical changes brought about by destruction, as in Laurence Binyon's lines:

> The August sun is ghostly in the street
> as if the silence of a thousand years
> were its familiar. All is as it was...
> ...What were windows, mere
> gapings on mounds of dust and shapelessness.
>
> (*The Ebb of War*)

But it goes deeper than this. A critic needs to think about the feeling of time having stopped in that mass sacrifice of a young generation. There was a feeling at the time that the young men were somehow meant for death. This thought was expressed by countless writers at the time. In that climate, the past becomes loaded with a sense of the sacred, timeless even, with a great deal of rhetorical, heightened language in use.

In this sense, the one great and significant event of a man's death in sacrifice for peace and freedom takes on a place in the cycle of the past seasons, the natural life of man in the landscape, as in Binyon's *The Sower*:

He scatters seed in a quick, deliberate toss,
The immemorial gesture of Man confiding
To Earth, that restores tenfold in a season's gliding...

This language of the seasons and the land is used richly and subtly in countless war poems of this period. The vocabulary of farming and husbandry is often used in ways which indicate double-meaning and layering of references. As you read, be aware of this.

Youth and the past

This almost mystical feeling for the immediate past as well as the distant past also relates to the statements made about youth in the poems. The majority of the casualties were very young men, many in their teens. E. A. Mackintosh's lines sum it up:

Take your risk of life and death
underneath the open sky.
Live clean or go out quick –
Lads, you're wanted. Come and die.

(*Recruiting*)

But creative use of the past and the state of youthful sacrifice is seen most notably in the poems of Sassoon, and his narrative poem *A Working Party* (studied fully in Chapter 6) illustrates this very clearly. The young man who dies is explained by means of his past life in contrast to the moment of his death:

He was a young man with a meagre wife
And two small children in a Midland town;
He showed their photographs to all his mates,
And they considered him a decent chap...

Notice how the adjectives 'meagre' and 'decent' add irony to the fact of his honourable yet needless death. But also, that the humdrum was transmuted in the 'glorious' opportunity to die for one's country, or so the thought went at the time.

Contrasting men and nature

An excellent example of how nature was used as a strong presence in the landscape of war is in Edward Thomas's poem *As the Team's Headbrass* (analysed closely in Chapter 7). The poem concerns a conversation between a man and a ploughman, and after talk of war and possible death at the Front, the narrator of the poem casually mentions that as they had been talking, some lovers had been into a nearby wood. The continuity of life is hinted at in terms of people as well as in the ploughing for new life, even as, in fields in France, the fields are 'killing fields'.

Some helpful guidelines on what types of writing about nature to look for are:

1. Traditional country people – often age and youth compared.

2. Simplicity and routine – compared with a drastic moment of trial.

3. Use of images based on rural life and plants.

4. Symbols – as in Thomas's poem the elm tree felled by a blizzard.

Georgian verse

It is relevant to mention here the great popularity of what has come to be called 'Georgian' poetry – a term mainly applied to the anthologies produced by the editor Edward Marsh and the publisher H. Monro. There were five volumes produced between 1912 and 1922. Rather unfairly, this poetry has come to be typified by often simplistic writing about the countryside, but several very talented poets contributed to these, including Sassoon, Blunden, Graves and Rosenberg. Edward Thomas's poem *Adlestrop* has come to typify this subject and attitude: a poem that contemplates the panorama of the English countryside from a railway station as the train stands idle. The important fact to grasp is that the poems often have the feel of being elegies – celebrating a simple beauty.

Features of Georgian poetry are:

▶ An interest in the English landscape.
▶ A prominence of more realistic diction about nature –
   compared with Victoria verse.
▶ A fondness for including rhymed and metrical verse.
▶ A direct style about ordinary subject-matter.

Figure 4.2. Features of Georgian poetry.

Nature comes to stand for many different things in the works of the war poets, but always be attentive to the applications of the word by different poets. It can range from the simplicity of the country back home to the elemental and ruthless force as expressed in William Blake's famous statement about 'Nature red in tooth and claw'.

Expressing 'England'

On the surface, the reader notices so much reference to England, in so many ways, when reading the poetry of the Great War, that it is easy to miss the layers of significance in this writing. As you read in preparing your essay, be aware of these usages and meanings of the word 'England':

▶ England as the place where 'home' is.
▶ England as something stable and reliable.
▶ England as a beautiful rural paradise.
▶ England as history.
▶ England as the formative part of the individual's identity.

At the heart of all these references is the contrast between the actual geographically-placed nation and 'England' as what we should now call an 'ideology'. That is, something with a whole range of established mindsets referring to the above things.

England and 'England'

Think about these contrasts:

England the place	'England' in the mind
Rural life and crafts	Noble gentlemanly morals
Church and belief	Code of honour
A modern economy-industry	Forests and fields
Small kingdom in Europe	Mother of a great empire
Stable society and order	The family/traditional life

Figure 4.2. Ideas about England.

In the minds and imaginations of the poets in the trenches, everything they missed about 'home' was potentially a part of this myth of what England was in terms of tradition and history. In the early phase of the war, poems such as Robert Nichols' *At The Wars* showed this evocation of 'home' in such 'Georgian' ways:

> But scenes and sounds of the countryside
> in far England across the tide:
> an upland field when Spring's begun,
> mellow beneath the evening sun
> ...An orchard of wizen blossoming trees...

Notice how this conveys home – choosing quintessential images of rural life. It is not the 'England' of the new towns and factories, for instance. At the same time as such lines were written from the Western Front, writers such as T. S. Eliot were writing about the fog-bound seedy night-scape of London and the refuse in the River Thames.

Using 'England' in essay themes

Acquire the habit of noting how images of England, in all the above senses, are incorporated into poems from the trenches. For instance, you might have a poem with roughly this range of subject matter:

1. Largely about a wartime experience. Refers to the landscape of the war.

2. But has about a fifth of the lines concerned with 'home'.

3. Most of the metaphors are about England and home.

Be aware of just what proportion of a poem is related to images of England. Even a simple word-count can be helpful, as, for instance, in Rupert Brooke's *The Rich Dead*, there is only one word with military application – the word 'Bugle'. In contrast, there are nine emotional adjectives about sacrifice, and thirty words referring to the place of England and home in this perspective on war. (This from a poem of only fourteen lines.)

Essay questions often ask you to write on how 'England' is used in the texts of the war poems. To summarise, these are the most commonly met types of references:

▶ as abstract nouns or concepts about morality
▶ as rural references
▶ as images of tradition and history
▶ as a place where there is life and new growth, instead of death and destruction.

Metaphors from the trenches

One of the best ways to bring all this together in an essay is to understand how to discuss and summarise the imagery of 'England' in a poem or a poet's work. A typical example is in the poem *This is No Case of Petty Right or Wrong* by Edward Thomas. The thinking as the poem develops goes through these stages:

1. The first nine lines state that the war is a significant confrontation which involves no strong personal anti-German feelings on Thomas's part. Yet he must decide.

2. Lines ten to eighteen state that from the horrors he dreams of a new, fresh England and imagines the perspective of history on this social change.

3. Finally, he leads to his conclusion with:

> I am one in crying, God save England, lest
> We lose what never slaves and cattle blessed.
> The ages made her that made us from the dust.

To the final thought that England is feminine, a 'She' and that all combatants must love her and all she stands for.

If we summarise the imagery here we have:

(a) The metaphor of war as a 'cauldron' leading to 'weather wise and gay' in England.

(b) The vision of a ruined land with 'ashes' and 'dust'.

(c) Finally, England personified as a woman:

> She is all we know and live by, and we trust
> She is good and must endure...

In writing your essay, or assembling notes before you write, list and summarise the images and how they relate to the various conceptions of England discussed above.

Poetic diction

At this point, remember that so many of the soldier-poets were young officers, upper or middle-class men with classical educations. They were well read in the classics and knew Standard English – the English of the grammar books and of Oxbridge – but they had no knowledge of or respect for non-standard forms of English such as would be spoken by the 'Tommies' – the ordinary private soldiers in the war. This piece of social history leads us to a fascinating insight into the diction of the war poems. Diction is a term used of the vocabulary of a poem. It refers to the word selection involved, and also to these factors in the words making up a poem:

1. The abstract or concrete quality of the language.

2. The general or specific nature of the words.

3. The Latinate or Anglo-Saxon basis of the words.

4. The use of non-standard forms of words.

5. The proportion and importance of stylised 'literary' diction.

It will be useful to practise this on a short poem such as Ivor Gurney's sonnet, *Pain*. All the poem does is simply focus on the greyness in the landscape of the trenches, and there is a reliance on most of the traditional uses of poetic diction, particularly the Latinate and abstract. Whenever these are used, the reader has important clues about how realistic and authentic the poem is likely to be. *Pain* sets out to show the suffering around Gurney, but also to be candidly realistic and direct about the varieties of pain around him in battle. For this reason, Gurney relies on specific instead of general words, and uses few Latinate or abstract words. That is, he wants to be descriptive of what is actually before his eyes, as in:

> Or horses shot, too tired merely to stir,
> Dying in shell-holes both, slain by the mud.
> Men broken, shrieking even to hear a gun.

Notice here that every single word is of Anglo-Saxon origin – 'slain' not its Latin equivalent 'destroyed'; also, most of the words have only one syllable (monosyllables). A simple way to see these differences is to think about pairs of words like this:

> work – labour
> fear – terror
> above – superior

The first words are of Germanic origin and the second words are of Latin origin. The effects in poetry are generally to be more direct and accessible. In war poetry, the subject is often elemental, basic and universal. Words such as 'pain' and 'death' will have the desired direct effect.

The imagery in the poem is minimal, but rhetorical, as in: 'The amazed heart cries angrily out on God' or plain metaphor even on the edge of being a cliché, such as: 'An army of grey bedrenched scarecrows in rows'.

A matter of sound effects

The other notable feature of war poetry in this context is in the attempts to give the words qualities of sound which will convey the 'feel' of the terrors of combat and add to realistic effects. This will be examined in more detail with reference to Wilfred Owen in the next chapter, but at this point, notice the categories of words which do this:

1. **Onomatopoeia** - the words which mimic the thing they describe: examples are 'caw', 'neigh' and 'screech'.

2. Clusters of similar sounds which convey a setting: called **alliteration.** Examples are: 'and there is murmuring of the multitude' (Charles Sorley, *A Hundred Thousand Million Miles*) and 'On marching men, on' (Charles Sorley, *All the Hills and Vales*).

3. **Repetition and parallelism** in which statements are repeated or contrasted for an effect of sound, for instance:

   What of the faith and fire within us
   Men who march away
   Ere the barn-cocks say
   Night is growing gray,
   leaving all that here can win us;
   What of the faith and fire within us
   Men who march away!

In this poem Thomas Hardy wants the rhythm of a march, so he repeats phrases and parallels some phrases such as the first and last pairs of lines.

Tutorial

Progress questions

1. What are the common ways in which the war poets refer to the past?

2. List the main aspects of nature found in poems from the trenches.

3. Define the difference between England and 'England' in the mind.

4. What main contrasts of poetic diction apply to this extract from a poem by Charles Sorley (*A Call to Action*):

They girt their loins up and they trod
the path of danger, rough and high;
for Action, Action was their god,
'Be up and doing' was their cry.

Points for discussion

How may we distinguish between authentic, convincing use of metaphors and dead, flat ones?

Practical assignments

1. Find some recordings of poems from the First World War made by professional actors. Notice the differences in Standard English and dialect or slang diction – and how dramatic and realistic the results of this are.

2. Find poems which use a predominance of Standard English and conventional poetic diction. Compare them with the language used by Wordsworth or Coleridge a century before and look for similarities.

Study tips

1. Use a slang dictionary to look up the army slang you find in poems and keep a checklist of them. For instance 'Blighty' was the name for England, and so the phrase 'to catch a Blighty' meant to be wounded, so that you could go home for a while, away from combat. Note how many of the words you list were

used metaphorically like this.

2. Pick a poem at random and count the number of words which try to recreate actual sounds of war. Then note how general this is in the majority of poems.

5

Wilfred Owen

One-minute summary – For many years, Owen has been ranked as one of the most significant poets to have emerged from the group of 'poets from the trenches' in the Great War. His reputation has grown as time has gone on and the literature of this period has been revised, but his poetry still has a very high reputation. There are certainly going to be essays specifically on his work in your examination or coursework tasks. In order to understand his achievement, it is necessary to see exactly what kind of innovations he tried to make, how he changed after a famous meeting with Siegfried Sassoon in 1917, and how anyone writing on Owen's work has to be aware of his technical experiments, and also how his earlier reading of the English Romantic and Victorian poets had an influence on his war poetry. Owen also had a love of French literature and culture, and that is a vital fact, as it gave him a perspective on the war from beyond the shores of Britain. He was in France when war broke out. In this chapter you will learn:

▶ how Owen defined poetry and what influenced his writing
▶ how his writing changed after meeting Sassoon
▶ how to analyse and write an essay on a typical Owen poem.

Keats meets the twentieth century

Anyone reading the collected poems of Wilfred Owen (the latest edition edited by Jon Stallworthy) is certain to be struck by the number of poems he wrote well before the outbreak of war, and how derivative these are. In these early poems, the reader sees the Romantic influence, but also some of the features which became important later. One is the reference to other literature and to myth; another is his love of rather lush and rhetorical verse. In fact, his reading and taste in poetry was typical of many young men of his generation. He admired Keats, Shelley and Swinburne. But he also had an enthusiasm for European poetry.

Keats and Owen

Owen's reading of Keats involved the absorption of the ideas Keats had about the significance of poetry and of creativity. Owen, from a Christian, middle-class family, was meant to be a clergyman, and was a vicar's student for some time before he questioned Christianity. Keats's poetry offered some exciting elements to such an imaginative, intellectually curious young man:

▶ A deep interest in classical literature and myth.
▶ A belief in 'inspiration'.
▶ A concept of poetry as a high and refined art of a fine and sensitive mind.
▶ A conviction that poetry is a craft, to be learned through hard application to study.

In Keats, Owen found statements about poetry that confirmed his own desire to make it the creative centre of his soul; Keats believed that 'if poetry come not as easy as the leaves on the trees it had better not come at all' and that what was considered beautiful in form was 'a joy forever'. This partly explains Owen's interest in the formal and metrical qualities of verse.

When writing on Owen's war poetry, the reader needs to be aware of the Keatsian influence, as some of these attitudes persisted. In his early poem, *To Poesy* for instance, Owen has these statements:

A thousand suppliants stand around thy throne,
Stricken with love for thee, O Poesy.

and

No more is this my fervent, hopeless quest –

> To stand among the great ones there, to meet
> The bards of old and greet them as my peers.

This attitude of seeing poets as a brotherhood is seen in his friendship with Sassoon, and earlier in his life, with the French poet, Laurent Teilhard.

The Keatsian influence in war poems

As you read, notice these kinds of juxtapositions, where Owen mixes the strong realistic language of immediacy with the conventionally poetic diction of the Romantics:

> Teach me for speechless sufferers to plain,
> I would not quench it. Rather be my part
> To write of health with shaking hands, bone-pale...
> (from *The Poet in Pain*, written 1917–18)

Notice the words 'plain', 'quench' and 'bone-pale' – all could be found commonly in poetry of the Romantic period. The word 'plain' is notably so, being related to 'complain' but that word means usually a lover's song or poem, hence giving the poem another depth of reference.

The early poetry

For the purposes of writing well on Owen's later war poems, then, note these features of his early, pre-war poetry:

1. Rich, sensual diction.
2. A tendency to write extended descriptive passages.
3. A rhetorical, over-stating element.
4. Use of Greek and Roman mythology.
5. Complex syntax in long, elaborate sentences.

Always be sensitive to Owen's tendency to interweave the poet of Keatsian sensibility with the hard, dour responses of the man who saw shell-holes, young men dying and all manner of physical and mental suffering. This fusion is at the heart of his unique poetic achievement. Yet, even in his early poems, Owen is capable of writing things entirely in line with current ideology about the sacrifice of young men in the war: 'O meet it is and passing sweet/ to live in peace with others/ but sweeter still and far more meet/to die in war for brothers.' (*The Ballad of Purchase Money*)

A young man transmuted to soldier

The dominant image we have of Owen is that of the idealistic, smart young officer, as on the cover of his collected poems, and in most anthologies on the Great War. But in his letters we have a portrait of a young man who gradually moved from being indifferent to the war to the experienced officer who led his men courageously and who, after suffering shell-shock, took 'time out' at Craiglockhart hospital near Edinburgh, to work on some of the most significant and original poems of the war. Becoming a soldier, he spent months being trained, at a range of venues across Britain, and eventually arrived at the front on 9 January, 1917.

When writing on Owen's work, always bear in mind the intellectual foundations of his mind which were part of his general attitudes to poetry. One central influence was his rejection of Christianity, and another was his affection for the florid, sensual diction of his reading as a young man – a Romantic impulse which saw poetry as something emanating from a spiritual core in the individual. A brief look at one of his poems written in the early phase of the war will prepare the way for the close analyses covered in this chapter.

This poem, *A New Heaven*, was written in September, 1916 and typifies the elements in his poetry before the radical meeting with Sassoon after Owen's neurasthenia developed and he was sent home to recover. The poem is a sonnet, with a rhyme-scheme of ABBAABBA in the first eight lines (the octet) and CDCDEE in the last six lines (the sestet). The octet contains strings of classical references to the afterlife and death, such as 'Lethe' and 'Styx', two rivers in Hades, the Greek afterworld, and 'Asgard', the home of the Gods in Norse mythology. But the title of the poem is from the Bible, Revelations 21:1 'And I saw a new heaven and a new earth'.

Also very interesting for future reference is the tone and the subject of the sestet, in which the young officer admits to the alluring vanity of having a uniform and the admired status of a soldier at such a time:

> To us, rough knees of boys shall ache with rev'rence.
> Are not girls' breasts a clear, strong Acropole?

'Acropole' the French for Acropolis, the fortified and highest part of a city, hence the famous acropolis in Athens, seems to suggest a link between the roundness of the hill. and women's breasts.

'Four Stages of Consciousness'

As you read as a critic, you should now be becoming aware that Owen's poetry is the best starting-point for studying this body of poetry because his writing reflects much of what the poet and critic Jon Silkin has called 'the four stages of consciousness' in the poetry of the Great War. Silkin's categories are as follows:

1. An early optimism and an idealistic response to the call for sacrifice. The writing is therefore predominantly concerned with patriotism, emotive diction and symbols of sacrifice. It accepts the militaristic codes already established in the Empire and in colonial warfare. Brooke and indeed early Sassoon would typify this.

2. Protest, anger and satire, most obvious in Sassoon, and hence his influence on Owen. This is intensely realistic and the writing calls on all the techniques of irony, sarcasm, satire and parody.

3. Compassion. Here, arguably, Owen takes centre stage, as he openly states that 'the poetry is in the pity' in his preface to his poems. This poetry is marked by a wider perspective on the setting and tactile feel of the experience of trench warfare.

4. Then, prophecy and vision – poetry insisting on seeing mankind and the aftermath of the war in radical, revisionary terms. Silkin refers to 'an active desire for change' in the poetry. He singles out Rosenberg as the representative poet in this respect. The characteristic is looking at human society and how it reached these unthinkable events.

(Source: Introduction to *The Penguin Book of First World War Poetry*. See Further Reading.)

The influence of Sassoon

On 26 June, 1917, Owen arrived at Craiglockhart Military Hospital near Edinburgh. Here he met Sassoon, who had been under treatment after his letter to the authorities saying that he would no longer fight in an unjust war. He had won the Military Cross and then thrown it into the river Mersey. At this point, he was writing, editing a magazine called *The Hydra*, and already had contact with the poet Robert Graves. But now Owen and Sassoon met and Sassoon's impact on Owen had these general effects:

Sassoon's influence on Owen
► A more explicit handling of the subject.
► Use of more direct diction.
► The adoption of a more distant voice and tone.
► A closer contact with the emotional centre of the experience.
► A more minute exploration of the human subject, through empathy.

Most of Owen's most successful and highly-rated poems were written in the year following that meeting in the hospital.

Example: *The Dead-Beat*
This is the ideal point at which to use a poem as a case study about Sassoon's influence on Owen. Owen wrote in a letter that he had been to see Sassoon and 'After leaving him, I wrote something in Sassoon's style...'. This was *The Dead-Beat*, a poem about a private soldier who has collapsed with sheer weariness and mental fatigue. The poem explores the range of attitudes held about the strains of the war by various ordinary combatants. I would like to use this as an example of what Owen has learned, and how he was beginning to experiment, before we look at two of his greatest poems.

The following is a useful way to work, taking the three sections of the poem and showing the technique and treatment of the subject as we progress:

Lines 1–8

An account of the man's collapse and mental condition. Then it uses his actual, pathetic words of 'I'll do 'em in...' Note the simple yet powerful *similes* at the opening: 'Lay stupid like a cod, heavy like meat'. These are intended to give the reader a plain but visually strong image of his mindless state.

Lines 9–14

In these lines, Owen uses the kind of slang and vernacular that gave Sassoon's satires so much bite. Other voices comment on the young man's home life 'It's not these stiffs have crazed him; nor the Hun'. So we have a glimpse of some 'home thoughts from abroad' which are very different from the sentimentalised ones we noted in Chapter 2.

Lines 15–19

These lines use the narrative voice in the third person 'We': 'We sent him down at last...'. This implies a voice of authority and command. Then all the diction, mixing slang with military and manly, tough words, drives home the ultimate irony of his death, where he is referred to as 'scum'. Note how there is no imagery in this last section: it is all matter-of-fact comment and that the suffering, insensate man has now become distanced by the use of the words 'stout lad' and 'scum'

All this shows clearly that Owen had learned to access the soldierly language of the harsh contact with boredom, mental stress, prolonged pain and physical endurance required of the men in that context. Owen had been blown up after leading his patrol into a shell-hole and that has caused his neurasthenia ('shell-shock') leading to his hospitalisation.

Time out and a new art

Wilfred Owen had taken some time out away from the front and had been given time to revise and revisit the scenes of his combat experience. The dramatic events that happened in January 1917 had now been moved 'centre stage' into his newly-established approach to writing. After all, in that month, his platoon had suffered extreme frost, one man had been blinded, he had settled in a dug-out in no-man's-land, and then been shell-shocked. For a young man in command, this was more than enough 'material' for new poetry.

But empathy was the central focus in the writing now. In poem after poem, he places the emotional centre on the suffering ordinary soldier and fully humanises the subject into a person held within a broader, universal struggle with a political confrontation very distant from the front line. Again, remind yourself that these men were not professional infantrymen, and that Owen was only just trained for command.

Textual study: Owen's themes

When you are tackling an essay on Owen's poetry, you need to think first of all about these three areas:

1. His overall themes and preoccupations.
2. His treatment of the subjects – from realism to vision.
3. His technique.

In terms of the themes, bear in mind that he had strong impulses towards writing a *didactic* poetry after the meeting with Sassoon. Didactic means written with a desire to teach or instruct. In other words, he already had the powers of acute observation and the need to express his emotional responses in verse; now, in 1917 he had a drive to educate, to think more of who was likely to read his poems. The irony is, of course, that his poems were not published in collected form until 1920.

The themes were now mostly linked to this need to give the reality of trench warfare to whoever might read at a point well beyond and outside the war – and that includes posterity, as all writers must have half a mind to their future readers. But in Owen's case, he seems to have seen that the subjects needing poetic treatment were now pressing ones: he had a personal impetus to release the truth as he had seen it into words and patterns of sound. The themes were therefore concerned with:

(a) Rewriting the immediacy of war experience.

(b) Giving the human element in the context absolute prominence.

(c) Setting the individual suffering within a wider context.

In an essay on Owen, Michael Schmidt said that, 'the deformed man and the pastoral landscape are given in the same rhythms' (Schmidt p. 152. See Further Reading.) This is a useful perception for anyone writing on Owen for examinations, as students and critics are in need of some help with these difficult poems. It is time to look at a typical poem from this group in detail. *Mental Cases* will illustrate some of these themes.

A productive method for explaining

Mental Cases, written in May–July 1918, is a poem with plenty of useful traits in terms of writing on Owen. It is typical of his writing when in the mood of writing rhetorically and powerfully with his usual mix of plain and stylised diction. Remember that *rhetoric* is a term used generally to define that style of writing which embellishes thought for a definite effect, such as overstatement or repetition.

Follow this process now, with the text to hand:

1. Read through first for the general meaning.

2. Read again and note the subject of each of the three sections. Write a prose summary.

3. Read one last time and note the stylistic devices.

Note that at this point it is helpful to give some guidance on the terminology used to write about poetry in general, so I will provide a list of usages to watch for, and then give brief explanations. This will give you a structure to build essay-arguments on. But never forget that you should always be guided by the words in the question, so if the question is about imagery, keep to that topic all the way as your thinking develops.

Checklist of stylistic devices/figures

Here is a checklist you could use when approaching any of the poems in the anthology you are using.

Group 1: Diction
▶ words conveying emotion
▶ specific terms in jargon
▶ consciously poetic words, rhetorical etc.

Group 2: Imagery
▶ metaphors
▶ similes
▶ personification
▶ catachresis
▶ patterned and sustained images.

Group 3: Syntax/word order
▶ sentence length and variation
▶ position of adverbs and adjectives
▶ breaks in normal expression.

To show these terms, we take a few lines from the poem:

> –These are men whose minds the Dead have ravished.
> Memory fingers in their hair of murders,
> Multitudinous murders they once witnessed,
> Wading sloughs of flesh these helpless wander,
> Treading blood from lungs that had loved laughter.
> Always they must see these things and hear them.

These lines are from the second section, in which Owen is out to shock, giving the revolting and authentic language of one who has witnessed such atrocities and wants to communicate this with some urgency. So we have these notes:

Diction – some high-flown rhetoric, as in 'ravished' but also very plain, bland language as in the last quoted line.

Imagery – personification in 'the Dead have ravished' and 'Memory fingers'. Here, the metaphor makes the abstract word into a sort of 'being'. Metaphors dominate in the first four lines, as in 'Memory fingers in their hair of murders.' A metaphor speaks of one thing in terms of another, so when reading and writing on metaphors in poetry, always look for lines in which the poet is searching for similarities and contrasts in terms *of what does not literally happen*. That defines a metaphor: it reads like something that could not actually be so, but is imagined, as in 'whose minds the Dead have ravished'

Also, we have *a conceit*: this is a bizarre and strange image which often breaks all conventional use of language, for example, the second line could be a conceit. A similar concept is a *catachresis* (see the glossary).

Syntax and word order – also interesting: notice the words 'these helpless wander' and ask yourself what different meanings the phrase could have. In that way you will notice that 'helpless' can be a noun or an adverb. Also, notice how the last line (and a new sentence) begins with an adverb of time, 'always', used in the unusual position of coming before the subject, 'they'.

Follow this checklist in the three groups and you will always have a structure for your essay.

Mental cases examined

Section 1 asks questions. The figures described are like inhuman shapes in purgatory, outside life, somehow. It starts the poem with a sickly, vague vision of unease and despair.

Section 2 describes, in horrendous detail, the landscape of hell from which these figures emerge. The nouns are strong enough to suggest this hell, without further adornment: 'carnage', 'sloughs of flesh', 'murders' and 'blood'.

Section 3 again simply describes the abnormal behaviour of men under pressure, and the extreme mental anguish of being within such a terrible conflict. The description is reminiscent of descriptions of maltreated inmates of lunatic asylums in the early nineteenth century: 'Thus their hands are plucking at each other' and so on. Today, we would have medical terms to explain the stress-centred movements of these wretched men.

A closer look at the diction provides another dimension to Owen's skill with words. In the last section, there are three compound words (hyphenated) as if he is trying desperately to say everything rather than not enough: so much is the spectacle almost 'beyond words'.

Above all, the poem illustrates Owen's growing themes as listed above, mainly in his need to write a didactic poetry. As here, in which the poem asks and answers questions. The first questions in section one could almost be the emotive rhetorical questions we hear on a voice-over of a gritty documentary for television today.

Close analysis: *Dulce Et Decorum Est*

Now we come to perhaps the most well-known and representative poems from Owen at this time. Read the poem in your anthology, and then look at the following analysis. This takes you through the poem as if you were compiling an essay-plan.

After you have read and written your own notes as in the model above for *Mental Cases*, compare this with the following:

Title
This Latin phrase is taken from the Roman poet, Horace's line meaning 'it is sweet and fitting to die for one's country' and comes from Horace's *Odes* III ii 13. So the poem starts with what is going to be a powerful irony by the time we reach the closure.

Section 1
This begins as if we are reading a narrative, with a description of men on the move, towards some destination, But they are barely 'men' at all – the words used demote them to creatures bewildered by the awful physical environment of mud. They are lame and blind.

Section 2
The tempo suddenly changes with an abrupt snap of 'Gas! Gas! Quick, boys!...' and the verbs used all convey panic and confusion. The central image of 'An ecstasy of fumbling' is loaded with implied meanings. 'Ecstasy' is usually a word used of extreme joy

and delight – it is even a religious word used of a transcendental experience. But here, paradoxically, it is linked to fear. One man fails to get his mask on. The image of 'As under a green sea, I saw him drowning' conveys the perception and the victim most dramatically, with a real economy of language.

Section 3
These two lines are isolated for potent emphasis. Note how it expands on the idea of a 'dream' and the three continuous verbs stress the desperate movements and sounds of a person dying in agony.

Section 4
The poem goes towards its closure with a tough and ironical address to readers who might potentially be imbued with the patriotic ideals implied by the title, and therefore, the horrific account of the death (the 'froth-corrupted lungs' etc.) adds to this irony. Notice that the whole of this last section is just one grammatical sentence, and so the reader waits a long time for the finite verb (main verb) 'tell' and the adverbial phrase 'with such high zest' following. In this way the twist of the title's application to military life is stressed with effective irony.

Dealing with essays on Owen: *Strange Meeting*

You now have a useful template from which to work when writing essays on Owen, but we cannot move on without a look at another side of his work: the visionary. You will be expected to be aware, when writing essays on Owen's work, that he reached for a whole range of amazingly original standpoints from which to view his subject of the war landscape. In one poem he even imagines watching the battlefield like a distant figure well beyond the reality of the trenches.

Strange Meeting is one of his poems which goes into an impassioned perspective of reconciliation, appeal for brotherhood, and a revision of how we are asked to see humanity within such horrors as warfare. Owen imagines that he has gone from the battlefield to some 'profound dull tunnel' and there he meets, in the midst of this hellish vision, the ghost of the enemy he killed. He speaks to the man, and the main riposte of the drama in the poem is a heart-felt account of wasted young life:

> ... Whatever hope is yours,
> Was my life also; I went hunting wild
> After the wildest beauty in the world,...

Then there is a switch to the future tense: 'Now men will go content with what we spoiled,...' So in one sense, the poem shows an aspect of Owen that suggests other ways in which his writing may have gone had he lived. It deals with huge political and social issues, yet the Romantic diction, persisting from his Keatsian days, is still a part of the argument:

> Then, when much blood had clogged their chariot-wheels,
> I would go up and wash them from sweet wells,

And, indicative of the change in Owen, the final image is given in stark, active, Saxon words:

> I am the enemy you killed, my friend.
> I knew you in the dark:...

Tutorial

Practice questions
1. Contrast the early and later poetry of Wilfred Owen.

2. What is the evidence that Owen was always interested in experimental rhymes?

Discussion points
How has a knowledge of the meeting with Sassoon helped you to understand Owen's poetry?

Practical assignments
1. Research the use of gas in the Great War. For instance, it was

used by Germany, France and Britain, and Germany used 68,000 tons. Check on mustard gas and ask yourself how much this knowledge helps you to understand *Dulce Et Decorum Est*.

2. Re-read any Owen poem written after the meeting with Sassoon and then look at other accounts of the meeting, such as you will find in Sassoon's memoirs or in a novel by Pat Barker, *Regeneration* (1991). See Further Reading for full details.

Study tips

1. Read Owen's poems looking for one specific technique each time. For instance, notice how being alert to where he places adverbs and adjectives affects the power of the overall images. *Note*: an adverb describes a verb – he ran *quickly*. An adjective describes a noun – a *red* house.

2. Compare a straightforward metaphor with a conceit to be sure you see the difference.
   metaphor = 'I see men far below me where they swarm'.
   conceit = 'picking at the rope-knouts of their scourging; snatching after us who smote them brother'.

   In a conceit, apparently very different ideas are brought together with a certain shock and force, making the reader work harder to wrestle some coherent meaning.

6

Siegfried Sassoon

One-minute summary – Siegfried Sassoon has come to represent the satirical edge on the poetry written by the soldier-poets of the Great War. His work will certainly be represented in the anthology you are using on your course. Of particular interest here is that Sassoon's career during the war years shows very clearly the change from patriotic zeal and idealism to hard and bitter questioning about the continuance of the war. After looking at Sassoon's compassionate realism, we look at the biographical background you need to know, how his poetry changed to become fiercely satirical, and what knowledge of poetic technique is required in order to write well about Sassoon's work. In this chapter you will learn:

▶ the features of Sassoon's deep attachment to poetry and to England
▶ what to look for in Sassoon's poetry as it changed
▶ how the perspective on 'home' deepened in the war poetry of 1917–18.

Knowing about the 'Mad Jack' image

Sassoon's poetry is easier to understand if you know a basic amount of biographical information about him. This is because he was meticulous in his keeping of diaries during the war, and he was involved in a scandal, caused by his own bold letter of protest to the government. He was from a countryside culture, reared in fox-hunting and horsemanship; he enlisted as soon as war broke out and was soon in action. His early writings show a young man committed to courage and sacrifice. His war diaries record his earnest thinking about religious questions and his poetry often has this undercurrent of Christian themes.

'Mad Jack'

Sassoon was often brave and foolhardy, and in June, 1916 he was awarded the Military Cross for gallantry in action, after leading an attack on a trench position and taking it. Even in his last action, after returning to the war in 1918, he was shot, grazed in the head (by a bullet from one of his own men). He developed a reputation for recklessness and so his nickname was established. This aspect of his personality is at the heart of his turning against the war when he wrote his famous letter of protest to parliament in July, 1917, pointing out the folly of the war being sustained not for good causes but for sheer aggression. It was read in parliament, and eventually, he was considered to be in need of psychological treatment and sent to Craiglockhart, where he met Owen, as recounted in the previous chapter.

Notebooks, experience and poems

We have a large amount of material from Sassoon about the composition of his poems. He wrote accounts of the events behind many of the poems, so we have help in interpreting these. The important point to consider is how he saw the way to create the necessary realism. His often rash and passionate nature comes through in his diaries, and this helps critics to write about the tone of anger and disgust often directing the poems. A typical example is *A Subaltern*, written after he had learned of the death of his friend, D. C. Thomas on March 18, 1916. In this poem he uses several techniques which were to become hallmarks of his style. Some of these are:

1. Use of direct speech, as in the last two lines:

    'Good God!' he laughed, and slowly filled his pipe,
    Wondering 'why he always talks such tripe'.

2. The use of authentic vocabulary from military contexts, as in the words 'crumps'.

3. The sharp juxtaposition (placing side by side) of contrasting detail, as here, where one line is about rats scampering 'across the slime' and then the gentle, calm lines about cricket in the opening few lines.

Shock and writing 'on the edge'

The 'Mad Jack' image perhaps sits well with the element in his work which insists on giving the reader sickening realistic details about death and dying, but he often does this as part of giving a fuller picture of an incident, as in *A Night Attack* in which he mentions both English and German soldiers caught in the fields of death. Lines such as:

> Then I remembered someone that I'd seen
> Dead in a squalid, miserable ditch,
> Heedless of toiling feet that trod him down.

But it becomes clear by the end of the poem that Sassoon is mixing imagery and physical revulsion to show how, in a grim way, the dead became part of the hellish landscape.

Understanding his satire

At this point, as satire is so central to Sassoon's work, there is a need to explain and define the term. The fundamental nature of satire is writing that attacks or ridicules wrong, evil or folly in its literary subject. Thus, Sassoon writes powerfully about the apparent heartlessness and blundering of the generals in his poem, *The General*, or he writes with irony and sarcasm about the distortions of truth in *Suicide in the Trenches*.

Satire may be directed at institutions and philosophies:
Example: 'They' against the paradoxes of Christian belief.

Satire may highlight hypocrisy:
Example: 'The hero' – about falsifying events.

Satire may be against indifference:
Example: 'The general'.

Figure 6.1. Varieties of satire.

It is often said that satire does not pinpoint individual targets but mostly expresses its criticisms at the general or impersonal elements in a situation; so, even when satire is social or political, for instance, it is rarely firing arrows at specific people. In Sassoon's case, in your essays you will need to differentiate between his subjects, as sometimes they are broad, national concepts such as 'honour' and at other times they are about the lies told at home about the nature of the conflict.

An example
The best way to illustrate this is to provide a clear example of Sassoon's most common satirical subject: *Died of Wounds*, which concerns the anger felt at the military terminology used in statistics and casualty figures. In only 12 lines, the poem succeeds in making the term 'slight wound' used in the last line a powerfully satirical statement.

> The first four lines use two rhyming couplets – eyes/sighs and fell/well. Subject – the patient's troubled voice in the ward.

> The second quatrain uses the rhyme scheme CDDC. The utterances of the suffering man dominate. In the night he rants as memory torments him.

> The final quatrain returns to rhyming couplets with the rhyme scheme of EEFF. The narrator is introduced: 'I wondered where he'd been...'. The complaining stops when the narrator awakes to find the man dead.

The technique is very simple but effective: Sassoon layers his poems with references to the tiny particulars of a scene, mixing talk and description, but then he opens out the theme to broader and more consequential things.

Close analysis: *Glory of Women*

When you answer essay questions on Sassoon, use this framework:

1. Summarise the themes and preoccupations of the poem.

2. Mention any relevant biographical information.

3. Discuss the different elements in the poem: diction, speech, satirical subject.

4. Define the satirical subject within the broad nature of Sassoon's work.

Reading the poem
First, look at the form and structure of the poem. Note these aspects:

It is a sonnet. It has 14 lines, with a rhyme scheme of ABABCDCDEFGEFG. Technically, this breaks down to these parts:
2 quatrains using alternate rhyme
a sestet (group of six lines with a rhyme scheme).

Also, notice that the metre is iambic pentameter – that is five metrical feet with the stress on the second syllable of each foot, thus:

You make us shells. You listen with delight
–   / –   / –   / –   / –   /

(N.B. – / means an unstressed followed by a stressed syllable.)

If you are not sure of these metrical beats, then just memorise these basic, and most commonly found metrical feet in English:

– / is an **iambic** foot   / – is a **trochaic** foot

– – / is an **anapaestic** foot   / – – is a **dactylic** foot.

This simply gives the poem a feeling of a certain tone and rhythm to match the feeling underneath.

Second, summarise the development of the thought.
First quatrain – addressed directly to women in general 'You'. All concerned with the glamour of martial heroism.

Second quatrain – tackles the paradox of adoration of dashing stories and ritual mourning.

First three lines of the sestet – how women are indoctrinated back home, about the myth of the indomitable British 'Tommy'.

Second three lines of sestet – a brutal image of a dead German and his imagined mother at home.

Finally, relate the subject to larger issues about the war and Sassoon generally.
For instance, the poem manages to interweave three threads of thought:

1. the 'back home' myth about the nobility of suffering and war;

2. the vicarious thrill of playing a part 'You make us shells';

3. the common humanity of people on both sides, and therefore –

4. the ultimate paradox of the brainwashed English women, never thinking about their German counterparts and what they share rather than how they are opposed.

From particular to general
Therefore, *Glory of Women* is an excellent example of how Sassoon's satirical perspective on the conflict brings together a civilian, non-combatant context with that of the front line, and also clashes the particular experience of fighting in the trenches or making munitions in factories at home with the reality of the horrific death in the last line:

His face is trodden deeper in the mud.

Putting all these thoughts together provides you with a very effective essay plan, and you can build up your structured essay from this, moving from (a) a description of style and language to (b) general statements about Sassoon's stance on the war and on his subject.

Writing on Sassoon: A typical question

It's time we looked at a typical examination question on Sassoon, so here is one that might be asked about his satirical poems:

Sassoon's great weapon is irony. He uses it notably successfully against those who have power in warfare. How far do you agree?

A workable approach to questions on set writers is to break down the aspects of the subject in the question. For instance, here, you are being asked how far you agree with two statements. The first one is about irony in general in his work, and the second is that Sassoon's ability in this mode when dealing with politicians and generals etc., is especially well done.

Acquire the habit of building your literary essays in this way:
Question 1 – What definitions do I need?
Answer – I need to explain irony and also Sassoon's use of it.

Question 2 – What texts shall I use for reference?
Answer – Two poems in reasonable detail and perhaps two other brief quotes.

Question 3 – How do I use the references when I discuss poems?
Answer – Briefly and always with relevance to the point you make.

Using quotation and reference
If and when you refer to a part of a poem for discussion, do it by incorporating the quote into your argument. Two sensible ways of doing this are:

1. A quote to support a general statement:
    e.g. Sassoon often uses physical description of people when they are his satirical target, as in the opening of *Base Details*:

    > If I were fierce, and bald, and short of breath,
    > I'd live with scarlet Majors at the Base,

2. A short phrase quoted within your sentence, thus:
    Sassoon often uses words to convey the physical revulsion of touch and sight in his accounts of the battlefield, as in 'The rank stench of those bodies haunts me still' (*A Night Attack*).

A paragraph to illustrate an argument

Let's take an example of how to develop a point in the essay title above. Your essay will have three sections:

First, take the key words in the question and define/discuss them. Here, they are 'irony' and 'successfully'. The first word needs explanation, and the second needs to be used as a measure of Sassoon's poetic practice.

Second, state how you intend to argue regarding the question, and use at least three textual references with each of three central points you make.

Third, end by stressing what your argument has been and how it relates to the question you were asked.

Here is a typical paragraph from the middle section, in which you use a textual reference. You are discussing the poem *Base Details* in which Sassoon directs his indignation against generals who are not at the front:

> Sassoon often writes with a tinge of bitterness about the military hierarchy, often giving them particular things to say so that their attitudes are dramatised for us. In *Base Details* for instance, he imagines 'scarlet Majors' safely 'at the Base' and away from the action, expressing regret at the deaths of young soldiers. He describes their lifestyles as being gross and indulgent, 'Guzzling and gulping in the best hotel' well away from seeing the horrific suffering the infantry is undergoing. Sassoon gives his satirical diction added power by making the generals' everyday slang words seem cruelly unfeeling. They refer to the war as 'this last scrap' and say that 'I'd toddle safely home...'

Defining terms

At the opening of your essay, you should define and qualify the key terms in the question. In this sample question, for instance, 'irony' needs to be discussed in a general way, to prove you know its meaning, and then explained in the way Sassoon uses it.

Explain with a brief example, as in:

> Irony is generally understood as a way of writing that reverses the expected meaning, as when generals are written about as

behaving like brutes and having no admirable moral qualities. Or, in more subtle usages, as in *Died of Wounds*, words and phrases may be used ironically when they clearly refer to a lie or a distortion (as in the last line of that poem).

Tutorial

Practice questions
1. Explain how a knowledge of Sassoon's life may be helpful in critical essays.

2. What do you understand by the term 'satire'?

Discussion points
1. How can a poet make use of dialogue and spoken words as satirical tools? Give examples.

2. What are some of the ways in which a poet can represent working-class or regional speech, as in the poems using slang? What does this add to the overall impact of a poem, and is there a risk of such writing becoming parody? You might like to think about what stops a poem from handling a serious subject in a convincing way.

Practical assignments
1. Read an extract from Sassoon's *War Diaries* (see Further Reading) and compare his notes with the poem written from the experience.

2. Write a list of clichés used about the Great War from the 'Home Front' and note how these are used by the poets.

Study tips
1. Keep up the habit of reading a poem several times before you attempt to write about it.

2. Write notes after your second reading, making sure you understand difficult words.

3. Try not to write too much around one text. This can be confusing when you re-read later.

4. When reading poetry, always look for words which may have a range of possible meanings, as in Sassoon's title *Base Details* in which the word 'Base' clearly has two meanings, one literal (the generals are at the base) and one satirical, 'base' meaning low or immoral.

7

Edward Thomas and Isaac Rosenberg

One-minute summary – Thomas and Rosenberg are both important poets and you are likely to have essay questions entirely concerned with their work. But they represent very different approaches to the subject of war, and the basis of their work offers interesting contrasts. Thomas was an established writer from a literary community, whereas Rosenberg was a visual artist from a poor Russian immigrant family. This basic contrasts provides plenty of useful thinking about the whole spectrum of potential standpoints which may be taken up with regard to the Great War. It also opens up the subject matter from trench warfare to more reflective, philosophical lines of thought in Thomas, and new varieties of realism in Rosenberg. In this chapter you will learn:

- ▶ how to write about Thomas's unique personal attitude to his war experience
- ▶ what aspects of writing technique emerge in their work
- ▶ how to understand the relationship between Georgian poetry and the war.

Knowing personal responses

In turning to the poetry of Edward Thomas, you have to move from a context of writing which was totally immersed in the school and the academic study of poetry to the case of a committed, well-published writer who had only recently begun writing poetry just a few years before his death. Whereas Owen, Sassoon and Brooke had experienced college or university and had concentrated on poetry, Thomas had been writing prose works in order to support his family (he had married in 1899 at the age of 21). Reading and writing about his war poetry, therefore, depends on having an understanding of his circle of friends, in particular the American poet, Robert Frost.

The personal and the public

Thomas was in his thirties when he joined up. He thought long and hard about the war, but he had been more deeply influenced as a writer by being in a community of writers who had settled in Dymock, Gloucestershire, in 1914. There he had been a biographer and reviewer moving among poets such as W. W. Gibson, W. H. Davies and Lascelles Abercrombie. But Robert Frost was the most profound influence. Thomas and Frost would walk for miles, notably in the Leddington area, talking poetry, and generally developing a close friendship. Thomas was led to reflect on his nature as a potential poet, and this meant thinking hard about his relationship to people, language, England and the countryside.

What Thomas learned from Frost

Frost was a countryman from New England who knew about farming and the land; he believed that poetry should not be hide-bound by rules of metre and patterning by syllables in any rigid way. He talked about the natural 'cadence' of speech and that poetry should try to access that rhythm in the voice. Thomas looked at his thematic material and his own genuine life-experience and began to write poetry. He wrote 170 poems in the years 1914–1917. He died on 9 April, 1917 from the effects of a shell-blast. But in that short time he had practised the theory he had talked about with Frost, and his war poems are remarkable in their easy and gentle reflection, mixing strong description with an acute ironical sense. He had learned these attitudes and approaches to writing poems:

1. To allow the voice in the poem to follow the natural cadence of expression.

2. To use the same dynamic language effects in poems that he had used in his prose.

3. To use colloquial language, even conversational lines.

4. To keep to the familiar and universal, but treat it with freshness.

Placing Georgian poetry

It is important to recall that the anthologies of Georgian poetry started by Edward Marsh contained in their view of poetry an attempt at providing a fresh, challenging type of writing, often using contemporary English life and culture as a focus. There had been a deep interest in the country for various reasons, and these need to be listed now as they will help you to understand why the springboard for much of Thomas's poetry is rural life and plain, working-class people.

The Rural Element in Thomas

► The countryside provided him with natural images which could be used and transmuted into startling metaphors.

► He had a deep love of England and a profound curiosity about the qualities of people leading simple, working lives.

► The threat of the new urban mentality and the growth of the suburbs and changes in the location of industry played a part in his attachment to small-scale society.

► The vocabulary of country life provided a poetic diction rich in sensuous, tactile and visual qualities.

► Relationships – in particular friendship – were more 'visible'.

Figure 7.1. Thomas's rural element.

In his famous poem, *Words*, Thomas says:

Out of us all
That make rhymes,
Will you choose
Sometimes–
As the winds use
A crack in a wall
Or a drain,

Notice how he relies on making maximum use of totally ordinary, monosyllabic words in the directing metaphor.

The general trend in Georgian poetry, via Frost and other friends, stimulated Thomas to write poetry using his already acquired knowledge of botany, rural life and tradition which he had gathered in his years of writing travel books and topography about England and Wales.

Viewpoints from a distance

Closely related to this is Thomas's fondness for locating the mood and focus of his war poems in the intensely personal area of the self, relationships and the bonds of love. So far, we have concentrated on trench warfare as the dominant subject in the poetry of the Great War. Now, with Thomas, notice this universal theme extended from a very personal poem, as in his *No One So Much As You* (probably written to his close friend, the poet Eleanor Farjeon in 1916). The first stanza explains this well:

No one so much as you
Loves this my clay,
Or would lament as you
Its dying day.

But in *Rain* we have a more direct war poem, mixing the atmosphere of the war with a blend of personal pain and a perspective of universal sharing of the predicament, with the opening lines:

Rain, midnight rain, nothing but wild rain
On this bleak hut, and solitude and me...

developing into these lines on the communal suffering:

Blessed are the dead that the rain rains upon:
But here I pray that none whom once I loved
Is dying tonight or lying still awake

The point to be aware of when writing about Thomas is that his own selfhood was troubled with depression and black moods (indeed he attempted suicide on one occasion) but that often he deals with emotions such as remorse and self-blame. His driving emotional impetus to be in the war was equally passionate. He is said to have picked up a handful of soil and said that he was going to the war 'for this'.

Close Analysis: *As the Team's Head Brass*

This poem is almost certainly in any anthology of poetry from the Great War. It is the poem that most clearly illustrates Thomas's war poetry. There are three main areas of writing to be sensitive to as you read and prepare to write:

1. The use of a story – like a casual anecdote between friends.
2. The use of objects and events as symbolic.
3. The use of conversation and colloquial language.

First reading
What happens?
The narrator of the poem chats to a man ploughing a field. A couple walk into the woods. The ploughman and the narrator refer to the distant war. The narrator sits on a fallen tree and then they discuss their involvement in the war. The worker says he would go if he could guarantee coming back – two friends have died there already, and so the tree has not been moved. The worker makes the philosophical statement about full understanding of events in life. Then the couple come out of the wood.

Second reading

Phase 1 – the observer and the action. Notice how Thomas uses the first person pronoun, 'I' to distance the actions, and also to keep the observer anonymous. It is the ploughman who does the movements and talks. The diction is very specific and the words such as 'fallow' (unseeded) and 'charlock' (a weed) help to give the experience an authentic feel.

Phase 2 – the conversation. Thomas makes the ploughman dominate by speaking forcefully but wisely. His talk is convincing in its plainness – 'One of my mates is dead.' But there is the use of seeming wild logic in 'I could spare an arm. I shouldn't want to lose/A leg.' This makes the topic of the war intrude harshly on what could be an idyllic scene in the *pastoral* tradition of a dialogue poem, or *eclogue*. The pastoral tradition often used country people and scenic settings to form pleasant images of rural England. Thomas is parodying this slightly.

Phase 3 – the last ten lines. The worker talks of the tree being still unmoved and goes from that to the stunning statement of 'If we could see all all might seem good.' This gives the reader a shock of revisionary perspective on any possible meaning the senseless war might have. The fact that an ordinary ploughman speaks the words adds a layer of irony.

Finally, the lovers come out of the wood, and the closing three lines the rhythm of the moving horses, notably in: 'I watched the clods crumble and topple over' as here the land is now active, dynamic, as the man was at the opening. Thomas/ narrator is, in contrast, passive, uninvolved and simply absorbing the irony of the lovers and the continuing life of the land. The powerful implication of the lovers in the poems adds a contrast so:

Layer 1 – the surface observed events of the ploughing and the immediate contemporary topic of the war.

Layer 2 – the notion of love and procreation the continuity of the life cycle.

Layer 3 – at the closure we inevitably compare the human

continuity and implication of birth and rebirth with the fecundity of the ploughed soil.

Of course, the whole poem, read as a war poem, becomes in many ways a great 'peace poem' as so many war poems are.

Comprehending word and image in Rosenberg

In contrast, the poetry of Isaac Rosenberg takes us back to the explicit depiction of warfare and the life of the trench soldier. But the perspective on the subject compares and contrasts strongly with Owen and Sassoon. This is largely because Rosenberg was initially a painter, having attended the Slade School in London before the war. His poetry has the dynamism and colour, the sensuality and 'noise' of a shocking image. Much of his perspective on art generally came from a mixture of his Jewish intellectual background, talking with poets and painters in the London cafés, and a dedication to the modern idiom in poetry. Like so many young poets at the time, he found a patron in Edward Marsh (who had also helped many of Thomas's friends).

Essential biography

Rosenberg was born in 1890 and grew up in the East End of London. He met with very little literary success, even after having booklet collections of his work privately printed. But he made some literary connections and managed to have a grant from a Jewish foundation to help him study art. Some of his work was exhibited, and he had a successful period as a lecturer on art in South Africa. He enlisted with the Suffolk Regiment in 1915 and then joined the King's Own Lancaster Regiment. He died on 1 April, 1918.

Key experiences

▶ In war experience, the *sheer poverty and deprivation of his life* in the infantry – after so much poverty in civilian life (he was always begging for money from friends).

▶ His interest in *printing and engraving* (compare William Blake).

▶ His ambition to write *poetic drama* (hence the importance of rhetoric and mythic writing).

Word and image – an example

A typical Rosenberg poem is *Break of Day in the Trenches* which is simply a meditation on a rat and its place in the battlefield, having 'cosmopolitan sympathies' moving from German to English lines. But Rosenberg makes the startling image of the rat a guiding principle for seeing man's predicament afresh, as in:

> It seems you inwardly grin as you pass
> Strong eyes, fine limbs, haughty athletes,
> Less chanced than you for life,
> Bonds to the whims of murder,

The purely descriptive contrasts of rat and man would normally lead to a logical progression, keeping a clear visual image, but instead, Rosenberg lifts the poem into a bizarre, surreal level in which a poppy is used as perhaps Dali would use it in a battlefield picture: 'Poppies whose roots are in man's veins'.

Rosenberg tends to start with a firm mental picture, then describe by means of sound and movement, before developing a stunning closing image.

Close Analysis – *Returning, We Hear the Larks*

The technique described above is neatly illustrated with reference to this poem. It simply recounts a group of men moving in the night, feeling sorrowful, then hearing larks singing. Rosenberg again plants his major, challenging images at the closure.

Structure

The poem has five stanzas: four of three lines and the final one of four lines. In a fully metrical poem, with end-rhymes patterned, this would be a *villanelle*. Rosenberg's poem uses the villanelle form to exploit a few effects of half rhyme, as in camp/sleep in stanza two, and then rhymes fully in the last stanza with tides/hides. The point here is arguably that the form itself is as vulnerable and fractured as the experience itself, as if Rosenberg implies that the chaos of war is reflected in the chaos of the poem.

Development of imagery

Stanza 1 – Abstract adjectives rather than images (as in 'sombre' and 'sinister').

Stanza 2 – The image of 'anguished limbs' places the strong logic of emotions being 'felt' by limbs. Equally, the track is 'poison-blasted'. So Rosenberg is purposely placing jangling, paradoxical words together.

Stanza 3 – The 'change of gear' as they hear the larks and we have a tone of joy. The metaphor of the night 'ringing' with the larks carries on the same kind of adventurous thinking as previously.

Stanza 4 – Now the first of a string of amazingly hard and appealing images is given. Death is personified, being able to 'drop from the dark'.

Stanza 5 – Finally, we have two images which each have a kernel of attractive unreason. They are both surreal – using the same method as a Surrealist painting. The first, 'Like a blind man's dreams on the sand' conveys the impossibility of larks (joy) in a battle. The second, '... a girl's dark hair for she dreams no ruin...' leads to a final line about the fear of deception and delusion in battle conditions, closing with the effective 'Or her kisses where a serpent hides' which evokes the Eden myth and a generally sensuous feeling of allure.

Diction

Notice Rosenberg's string of paradoxical contrasts:

(a) The human and the inanimate.
(b) The light and dark.
(c) The dead and living.

(d) The real and imagined.

Put together, these all make a clear example of Rosenberg's unique poetry on the war: a blend of the harshly realistic and the shockingly unsettling surreal – literally 'on-reality or above reality' – a technique that tries to show truth by overstatement and playing with the patterns of logical thought.

Tutorial

Practice questions

1. Look up the prose writing of Edward Thomas, and compare his nature writing with his poems.

2. How would you define personification? (check in the Glossary)

Discussion points

How far does an understanding of Georgian poetry help in reading the war poets?

Practical assignments

1. Read some standard villanelles (such as Dylan Thomas's poem, *Do Not Go Gentle into That Good Night* and compare them with Rosenberg's *Returning We Hear the Larks*.

2. Look for different examples of poets using emotional adjectives applied to objects or things without minds/feelings in war poetry. Consider the effects of this.

Study tips

1. Remember to take a poem stage by stage, and in Thomas's case, to watch how he uses the narrator, the 'I' of the poem. Notice when this is important and when it is eclipsed for a reason.

2. Read about the Dymock Poets (see Further Reading) and make notes on Thomas and Frost as poets wanting to use ordinary people in their work. Compare their methods with how modern writers do this.

8

Textual Studies and Examination Questions

One-minute summary – The chapters so far have been concerned with the main focus of the war as depicted in poetry – the conflict in the trenches. I have also spent most time and space on the major poets. But there are examination questions which ask you to have a wider knowledge, either of less significant poets or of themes concerned with topics other than the actual front line. Also, we have not yet itemised, stage by stage, the planning of essays and the reading of typical questions. In the following pages, I aim to introduce all these aspects. In this chapter you will learn:

- ▶ how to relate the work of some minor poets to wider themes
- ▶ which themes are important across the various poets' work
- ▶ how to plan an essay methodically
- ▶ how to interpret a typical question.

Including other poets: Ivor Gurney and others

Notice at this point that the themes that preoccupied the poets we have discussed so far were about suffering, the brotherhood of the battle, political subjects and the thoughts of home and England. We have not yet pinpointed some of the more specific aspects of this war as it affected people. One of the most commonly met subjects is sanity, shell-shock and the effects of war on mental health generally. The illness following shell-shock, or neurasthenia, was accompanied by shattered nerves, terrible nightmares, and difficulties in surviving as a 'normal' person doing everyday duties and keeping up social roles. The life and work of the Gloucestershire poet, Ivor Gurney, illustrates some of this.

Gurney's life and war experience

Gurney was born in Gloucester in 1890, and was a talented singer and musician. He wrote several songs as well as poems. At first, his poor eyesight kept him out of the army, but in 1915 he joined the reserve battalion of the 5th Gloucestershire Regiment. He served at Arras and was shot in the arm, and gassed at St Julien. He contemplated suicide in recuperation at home, and after the war he studied music again and lived without extreme problems until being placed in an asylum at Gloucester, and then London.

His poetry illustrates a quality not often found in the other poets we have read so far. His vision is one full of passionate and elegiac tones of loss and melancholy, as in *To His Love* is which he gives the voice of a civilian back home, lamenting the loss of a beloved, using a rhetorical style culminating in a shock at the closure:

> Cover him, cover him soon!
>   And with thick-set
> Masses of memoried flowers–
>   Hide that red wet
>   Thing I must somehow forget.

Gurney's emotive diction and unashamed use of techniques such as alliteration, abstract imagery and standard metrical forms all add up to simple but powerful statements about loss and parting, and he can also provide a transcendent vision going above and beyond the immediate horrors and sufferings of the war zone, as in *Photographs*, with the repeated celebration of fun and laughter alongside the pain:

> Smiles and triumphant careless laughter. O
> the pain of them, wide Earth's most sacred things!

Other poets and specific subjects

In your set anthology, you will find that lesser-known poets are represented, often with one striking poem that seems to say something notably unusual or off-beat. Examples might be Alan Seeger's *The Aisne* or Herbert Read's *My Company*. Seeger's poem illustrates the grand poetic diction and over-statement of the work in the early phase, and serves as a clear instance of the idealisation of the *esprit de corps* – the togetherness and sense of community in soldiers at war. His lines,

> There we faced under the frowning heights
> the blast that maims, the hurricane that kills;

This is an excellent example of the imagery making a natural landscape or feature into a thing with 'feelings' – it is called the 'pathetic fallacy' and is typical in that phase of the war.

Herbert Read's *My Company* which is a heart-felt tribute to that very *esprit de corps* at a later point in the war, when there was a certain amount of sad and proud reflection on the trials and pains endured. His words show the tendency for direct feeling to break down the covering of poetic style and embellishment – in short, the power of plain expression of feeling:

> My men, my modern Christs,
> your bloody agony confronts the world.

Using reference across several poets

Our glances at Gurney, Seeger and Read show how your wide reading, and sensitivity to other, less notably mediated voices from the war offer fresh insights. Brief references to their work, in contrast with the central figures, tells the examiner that you have read widely and thought in terms of comparison. Therefore, read and use these texts in these ways:

1. To show that a theme in a major poet is there in other, lesser known work.

2. To show contrasts in style and diction.

3. To be aware of perspectives from more central viewpoints.

Writing about metrical poetry

Although brief explanations have been given about poetic metre, this is a good point at which to consolidate the topic, and to give an account of the basic knowledge you need to include a brief discussion of metrical effects in an essay. But remember that it is not productive to write at great length on this. It is merely an explanation of verbal effects, so keep in mind this guideline: *write about metre only to show how it enhances the poem's theme.*

Metrical feet in English poetry in general and unstressed syllables are shown by –, and stressed syllables with /. So the word 'unknown' would be –/ and the word 'never' would be / –. A foot has either two or three syllables. There are four very common types:

Two-syllable feet	– iambic (stress goes – /)
	– trochaic (stress goes / –)
Three-syllable feet	– anapaestic (stress goes – – /)
Dactylic	(stress goes / – –)

The best way to show this is to take a stanza from Thomas Hardy's *Men Who March Away:*

In our heart of hearts believing	– – / – / – / –
Victory crowns the just,	/ – – / – /
And that braggarts must	– – / – /
Surely bite the dust,	/ – / – /
Press we to the field ungrieving,	– – / – / – / –
In our heart of hearts believing	– – / – / – / –
Victory crowns the just.	/ – – / – /

The point to note here is that the stanza shows why poets bother to use metrical feet and the patterns that emerge over the lines of a poem. When you read a war poem, look for the significance of metrical lines in these ways:

1. Does the metre add to the effect of the attitude to the subject?

2. Does the metre relate to the movement in the poem's subject or mood?

3. Is the metre used openly for a rhythmic purpose?

4. Or is it used subtly for more restrained effects of sound and mood?

Poems from the Home Front

During the Great War, almost a million women were employed in munitions factories, making bombs and bullets. Although this was the period of agitation for votes for women, no significant perceptions in how women established themselves in independent work, comparative to that of men, occurred until this war. But the poems written at home, predominantly by women poets, show the spectrum of attitudes thus:

Extreme patriotism—mere acceptance and comment—criticism

Some poems at home confront the issues of suffering, but many are about family relationships, the changes in gender roles and indeed often show much more directness and bias than the poems by soldiers. Some poems, like Jessie Pope's *The Call*, are forthright about their criticism of young men still at home:

Who'll stand and bite his thumbs –
Will you, my laddie?

But perhaps the most interesting is the angle they give on the battle. As we have already seen from the infantryman's point of view, the pressing topics were there for all to see – action, togetherness, sacrifice, suffering and death. But poems such as Janet Begbie's *I Shouted for Blood* make us think of the women's attitude to dying in battle:

Your wounds are ceasing to bleed.
God's ways are wonderful ways, brother,
And hard for your wife to read.

Reading some poems written in England give you a different perspective, and often help to clarify the attitudes writers such as Sassoon developed when their satire became increasingly bitter.

Planning your essay

If we now put together the additional material covered so far in this chapter, it will be noted that there is now enough material in several categories to prepare you for writing a successful essay on the war poets. These are the areas you need to know and apply when writing:

Macrocosm – the wider world:
– historical detail
– biography, where relevant
– poems from a distance (from the Front)

Microcosm – the battlefield:
– comradeship
– physical landscape
– metaphors of hell/purgatory
– suffering and death

Figure 8.1. Planning your essay.

The stages in planning your essay should be like this:

Question: Discuss the varieties of satire in the war poets' work, explaining which poets are most successful in writing satirical poetry.

Stage 1 – consider the question
The task is to be broken up thus:

(a) 'Varieties'. This is asking you to show that you are aware of a diversity of types by various poets.

(b) Words are needed to describe the different varieties – by styles/ differences in emotion etc.

(c) 'Successful'. This implies success in terms of literary merit, so your essay must show skill in writing, ways with language and form which excel in comparison to other work.

Stage 2 – select poems to discuss

Here, the purpose is to discuss poems showing the varieties, and to use comparison and contrast to show the unusual, the innovative and the most interesting and powerful in terms of what they set out to do.

Stage 3 – plan the argument

Use the following plan:

(a) Discuss and define the key words in the question.

(b) Stress that 'successful' is in terms of achievement in the degree to which the poem meets the objectives and has the desired effects on the reader, but is also about innovative, accurate and suitable language and poetic form.

(c) Go through at least two poems, comparing and contrasting their style and language.

(d) Make the conclusion with ample reference to the words of the question. Keep quoting the key words in the question throughout your essay.

Interpreting the questions

The main categories of questions on literature generally are these:

1. The work of a specific writer.
2. The skill of comparing two writers or works.
3. The writing itself and some aspects of background.
4. Specific detail on style and form.
5. Specific questions on themes and subjects.

Examples of questions

Question 1: To what extent is it accurate to say that Wilfred Owen was the most experimental and innovative poet of the Great War?

This question asks you to deal with grand, demanding concepts. So all you can do is compare him with others and stress his originality.

Question 2: Contrast the attempts to be brutally realistic in the work of any two poets.

Here you are given two key words, each one charged with difficulties of definitions, so you need to come up with some criteria of what make a poem 'realistic' and what 'brutal' implies.

Question 3: In what ways does a knowledge of poets' lives enhance our reading of the war poets of 1914–18?

You need to make brief references to one or two poets' experience and relate it to their work. For instance, a comparison of Gurney and Sassoon would show two aspects of the question – Sassoon's life being known through journals; Gurney's rather more complex life because of his mental instability.

Question 4: How are poems made to deal with reality in this war? Refer to at least two poets.

Here you should discuss, for instance, techniques of making a poem realistic and authentic, such as conveying the words spoken by men or the sounds of a bomb attack.

Question 5: This might be: Explain how the nature of friendship was written about in the poems from the trenches.

Here, there are a whole range of options, asking that you discuss perhaps three or four poems briefly, showing a variety of aspects of friendship. A good overall technique in questions like this is to list as many aspects of the key word as you can in your planning notes. For example:

Friendship:
> class difference
> slang language
> comrades depending on each other
> sharing hardship
> men being tested, etc.

Tutorial

Practice questions

1. Explain why the idea of 'madness' could be so important in understanding war poetry.

2. How does Gurney's poem *Photographs* differ from Owen's trench poems?

Discussion points

In what other ways did writers try to explain the stress of war experience? Look at some diaries and letters and compare them with the poems.

Practical assignments

1. Practise scanning a metrical poem. Just write the stress patterns next to the lines. Compare one in a regular, formal pattern with one which is more experimental.

2. Look at some poems by women writers in the anthology *Scars Upon My Heart* (see Further Reading) and find poems that deal with military experience. Compare the real with the imagined accounts of battle.

Study tips

1. Find some songs, posters, leaflets newspapers etc. from the period and compare their view of the war with that in the poems. For instance, a 1915 poster has a woman reclining, nursing a baby with the word ENLIST beneath.

2. Find advertising literature and imagery from the home front (see M. Rickards and M. Moody, *The First World War*) and

compare the visual images of soldiers with those in the poems.

3. Find some of Ivor Gurney's songs and notice the use of metrical feet in these, as compared with the more complex patterns in (say) Owen's *Anthem for Doomed Youth*.

9

Some Broader Perspectives

One-minute summary – In addition to knowing about the texts of the poems, there is a range of secondary knowledge necessary in writing essays on literature. Some of this is related to the period, and some of it to the general systems of ideas being mediated by politics and the media at the time. There are also some additional literary topics in the case of the poets of the Great War which merit separate attention. One of the most important of these is looking at the available first drafts of poems and seeing how these drafts emerged in the finished texts. It is useful to know something about how the war has been seen so far, and what the general critical opinion of the poetry is. In this chapter you will learn:

▶ how to select historical factors for use
▶ how to link the ideology of war to the writing
▶ how and when to use knowledge of critical views of the war writing
▶ how to relate drafts to finished poems for essays.

Poetry and historical factors

Obviously, in writing about a war that took place in the years 1914–18 entails a great deal of historical knowledge. But most of the general historical works available will necessarily contain massive amounts of information which will not be helpful to you in preparing and writing essays on the war poetry. However, there are certain elements of historical knowledge essential to a full and honest reading of the texts. The categories of 'knowledge' embrace some aspects which are factual, and others asking us to use the empathy discussed in Chapter 1. For instance, think about these categories:

▶ **Political history:**
  – causes of the war
  – conscription
  – propaganda.

▶ **Military history:**
  – battle strategy and leadership
  – armaments
  – fighting conditions
  – ancillary services
  – variety of servicemen and women
  – different arenas of war.

A glance at this list highlights the need to select, and to know which aspects of history are of most use to you. Here is an illustration of what I mean; supposing you are studying Owen's *Dulce Et Decorum Est*. You would need these areas of historical knowledge:

▶ The title – assumed knowledge of Latin in his readership.

▶ Military details
  – a knowledge of soldiers' clothes and gear
  – knowledge of the effects of mustard gas.

▶ Vocabulary – slang words or technical terms such as 'flares' or 'Five-nines'.

But note there is also the ideological knowledge needed to relate the irony of the title to the pervading view of noble sacrifice and how this had been made almost universal by the press and by advertising and campaigning.

A sliding scale of knowledge
With this in mind, a good way to work when putting together a general summing-up of a poet's work is to list the aspects of historical knowledge that is absolutely essential and to list these in your notes with the notes for each poet. This is worth doing for Owen, Sassoon, Rosenberg and Thomas, simply because most

questions are concerned with their work. Your list for a typical Owen poem might be:

▶ **Essential**
  – what duties an officer had
  – how he related to the trench duties
  – his dress and firearms
  – the nature of infantry combat.

▶ **Secondary**
  – wider politics
  – social history behind the conflict.

Whereas, for Edward Thomas, this would be different, as his life was very different. In fact, we have concentrated on the poems written on the Western Front, but there was also an Eastern Front and a conflict in the Dardanelles (in 1915). There was also a combat in the air and at sea. There were balloons involved and also tanks. Many soldiers were drivers (riding horses or driving vehicles). There were even cyclists and motor cyclists. But for reasons to do with the sheer intensity of infantry battle on the Western Front, the bulk of the poetry comes from that arena.

Understanding ideology in context

Absolutely crucial to a full understanding of this writing, however, is some serious reflection on the nature of the dominant ideology of the war at the time. An ideology is a belief system mediated to a large community, often by influential minorities or sometimes individual figures (such as the small Nazi party influencing German thinking in the Second World War).

An ideology is easy to see in retrospect but is often not perceived by people at the time, caught up in dynamics systems of propaganda. Ideology is therefore a set of ideas generated by a certain material or power-centred interest. For instance, it is essential to know something about the ideology behind the Great War in order understand Sassoon's attitude to the military leadership.

Ideology and its expression

In the context of 1914, there are various factors influencing the general attitudes of soldiers enlisting in the first great wave of volunteers forming Kitchener's army. But a broad comment based on the propaganda of the time would see an ideology of 'just cause'. After all, the political facts were:

(a) We were allied to France by the Entente Cordiale (1904).

(b) We had to defend Belgian neutrality (based on the London Treaty).

(c) We had been preparing for potential military confrontation with Germany for over fifteen years.

But, as literary critics, we need to see the expressions of these factors in terms that would have influenced the 'Tommies'. For instance, an advertisement for 'Binnacle' cigarettes in 1914 shows a young lady accompanied by a man in civilian dress and an officer. She is paying attention to the officer and ignoring the civilian. The officer is clearly smoking a Binnacle cigarette. A postcard of 1915 shows a Tommy lighting his pipe in the midst of battle. He smiles and his words are ' 'Arf a mo Kaiser!' He is the cheeky Cockney people would have seen on the London stage in social comedies back home.

Ideology in popular culture and poetry

Examples such as these are much nearer to the experience of the infantrymen under the command of the war poets discussed here. In the poems, the images from popular culture are often used, just as the men featuring in the poems are often working class people – the men openly influenced by the ideologies against Germany and pro-patriotism for 'England' in the abstract (as discussed in Chapter 1).

For instance, in the poem, *The Volunteer* by Herbert Asquith, the 'clerk who half his life had spent/Toiling at ledgers in a city grey' becomes a knight in shining armour, dying for honour, in a line of 'noble' confrontations in France, going back to the fifteenth century:

Nor needs he any hearse to bear him hence,
Who goes to join the men of Agincourt.

Here, the image of Agincourt, a battle in which Henry V defeated a numerically superior French army, hardly seems fitting in the context of 1914, but the spirit of knighthood, nobility and sacrifice is, of course, vague, muddled and paradoxically, powerful in popular culture – part of a massive ideology machine influencing young people to 'join up' and do their bit.

The ideology is both transparent (in the references made in many poems) and hidden (noticed obliquely through quotation or paraphrase. For instance, Sassoon can attack the dominant ideology very powerfully, as in *A Working Party* when he makes his doomed soldier a very ordinary man who has been made into a sacrifice in the war context:

He was a young man with a meagre wife
and two small children in a Midland town

and:

And always laughed at other people's jokes
Because he hadn't any of his own.

Which seems critical, but is, in fact, a profile of the ordinary man transformed by the war, despite the unheroic death recorded by Sassoon.

Basically, you are dealing with the pervading ideology of war whenever these aspects of the war occur in poems:

1. Sacrifice.
2. The brutality or inferiority of the enemy.
3. Language becomes heightened (rhetoric and hyperbole).
4. The mundane is transmuted into the heroic.
5. 'England' is mythologised and idealised.

Ideology, lying behind the thinking and feeling evident in the writing, is always central to war poetry, as wars tend to begin with ideals and morality, then tend to decline into stalemate, suffering and meaninglessness. Ideology provides a surface meaning, apparently clear and proper; then over time, it disintegrates and questioning develops into opposition.

Checking secondary criticism: established readings

In the study of any literary texts, the student always comes up against the various readings of the literature of any period or genre. There is always a body of established criticism, a constant attempt to 'place' a text in terms of how it compares with others, how it illustrates the period and so on. These established readings will change with academic fashion, and also change as new schools of critical theory come along.

But there are some broad approaches to criticism which will repay some thought now. In general terms, these are:

1. Textual – concerned largely with the verbal structures of specific poems.

2. Contextual – concerned with the setting: the historical, social and ideological factors, or also the biographical data available.

3. Intertextual – concerned with contrast and comparison, how similar subjects were treated by different writers.

All your literary study will in some way involve a variety of combinations of these aspects of reading and criticism. There are dominant, influential readings, and most anthologies summarise these (often in the introduction) but this is a good place to offer you a list of the well-established readings, so that you know what you are dealing with.

In terms of the Great War and the poetry from the trenches, these are the existing readings which have held sway but which are always open to discussion and debate. They are only the most widely-known and examined ones.

> **Statement 1**: This is a unique body of work in which the subject matter in some ways overcomes the actual poetic technique 'the poetry is in the pity'.
>
> **Statement 2**: This is the poetry of 'levelling' – a literature in which class and social different dissolves in the setting of common pain and trial.
>
> **Statement 3**: There are two or three outstanding poets, and a 'second wave' of minor poets.

Figure 9.1. 'Readings' of war poetry 1914–18.

Notice how all this implies that there has been a process of sifting and selection at work. The actual trench combat has taken the foreground, but these revisionary views have also been undertaken: women's poetry of the period has been re-assessed, notably in the excellent anthology, *Scars Upon My Heart* (see Further Reading); we have also gone through a period of influential gender criticism which has helped us to read the poetry freshly, with an awareness of the versions of maleness exhibited in the writing.

Majority and minority readerships

The point above about the 'major poets' being decided on by influential criticism is worth noting. Poets such as David Jones, author of a long and complex poem of the war, *In Parenthesis*, is regarded by many as the most outstanding poet of them all; yet Owen and Sassoon still dominate the anthologies. Ask yourself why this is. Some of these possible answers will help you when you write on Owen, Sassoon and the others:

1. Readers still want the accessible writing dealing with powerful emotions.

2. Readers still prefer largely descriptive, plainly realistic writing.

3. Critics and anthologists have always stressed the work of writers whose poetry explains the current ideologies.

As you read and note the realistic techniques, notice how there seems to be a 'league table' of writers according to some general criteria. Your anthology is probably based on this thinking, and such a line of thought, creating preferred texts and writers, is called a 'canon'. A canon is a body of texts taken to be representative of the best writing of a certain period, theme or genre.

Rebels

For instance, with the idea of an established reading providing a 'canon' of war poetry, notice how this is involved when you read a minor poet who has considerable interest – a poet like Ivor Gurney for instance – who is not mediated as being as 'important' as Owen and is not given the same space in a standard anthology. Asking why this is the case often opens up questions of the difficulty of the texts. The 'rebel' texts may be:

▶ poems containing complex syntax or vocabulary
▶ texts with innovative and challenging formal structures
▶ poems dealing with marginal experience.

For instance, check your anthology and see how many poems you can find that deal with areas of the war other than the Western Front. Note how many women poets are included.

Including discussion of writing drafts

Turning to another general area of interest for essays on the poetry of the Great War, there has been no mention so far of using your knowledge of early drafts of poems. We have several early drafts of poems by Wilfred Owen in the *Collected Poems* edited by Jon Stallworthy. I have left this issue until after the chapter on Owen, as it raises other point which will enhance your writing.

Why drafts?

A poet often uses a notebook for rough work and to note first impressions of subjects which may or may not shape into a finished poem over a period of time. Imagine Owen in the trenches, notebook in hand, reflecting on his observations *as they happen*. Sassoon did the same – he kept a war diary and often wrote a poem to follow up a prose reflection of something that had just occurred. A first draft of a poem is useful in our overall reading for these reasons:

1. It gives an insight into the process of thought behind the finished poem.

2. It shows exactly what has been rejected, and therefore gives clues as to the intention.

3. It gives an insight into word-selection.

4. It shows the gap between the actual closeness to the immediate experience and the writing structures.

An example

Owen's poem, *The Dead-Beat* shows this very well. As discussed previously, the poem is about a young man who is seen as a 'malingerer' and he is referred to as 'scum' by the doctor in the last two lines. There are several early drafts or part-drafts, and a few references will show how useful this is. For example:

line 6   – final draft has 'Or see the blasted trench at which he
              stared'
              earlier draft – 'Or see or smell the bloody trench at all.'

The changes have the effect of playing down the mental state of the soldier, giving a more restrained and bare account ('stared' has gone, and 'bloody' gives more of a sense of a simple curse).

Final two lines: final draft has – 'Next day I heard the Doc's
                   well-whiskied laugh: "That scum you sent last
                   night soon died. Hooray!" '
                   earlier draft has – 'Next day I heard the Doc's
                   fat laugh: "That dirt You sent me down last
                   night's just died. So glad!" '

The final draft has much more force in the brutal, indifferent condemnation of the dead young man. The doctor is drunk and he is given 'scum' instead of 'dirt' in reference to the man. It all gives a far more intense effect of tough satire on the lack of feeling involved.

How to use this material

Be aware of these drafting processes in the major poems of Owen and Sassoon. In addition to your course anthology, read some of the poems in the Owen *Collected Poems* and read Sassoon's *War Diary*, at least the first 30 pages. In your essay, try to use a few key allusions to very important changes – as above – in which Owen has clearly changed the tone of his satire quite radically. You might express it like this:

> Owen wrote several drafts of *The Dead-Beat* and it is clearly one of the poems with which he worked intently on making the callousness of the officer's attitudes come through very forcefully. The words changed in later drafting serve to intensify the vocabulary used to condemn the attitudes of the doctor in the final lines for instance.

Biography? Knowing how much to use

There is a massive amount of biographical writing available about the poets. The question arises: to what extent should you integrate discussion of this with your writing about the texts? A useful guideline is to look at the aspects of a poet's life which relate most closely to the work in terms of influence. But the whole idea of influence is hard to tie down, and often creative artists are unable to explain what influences bear on their work.

A productive idea in study skills is to write a full list of all the potential biographical experiences of a writer and ask which ones really do seem present in the writing. Here is an example from the life of Wilfred Owen:

Influences?
▶ Books read – formative reading.
▶ Experiences as a Christian – living with a Church of

England parson and experiencing 'Revivalism'.

▶ His Francophile culture, and life and work in France just before the outbreak of war.

▶ His adoption of the myth of heroism.

The list could go on, and so your most sensible ploy is to use biographical summaries, rather than the full and detailed definitive biographies. In this respect, for instance, Jon Stallworthy's biography of Owen has almost everything, whereas the summaries in the book by John Lehmann, *The English Poets of the First World War,* is more easily absorbed.

Biography or battle data?

There is perhaps a good argument in favour of giving time to the crucial information about the actual conflict than to poets' lives, on the grounds that it will help you understand the references and general conditions more comprehensively. A good example would be the information about very practical aspects of soldiering, such as the disaster at Gallipoli, in which there were immense losses of British and Commonwealth manpower. In a recent book edited by Tim Coates, for instance, *Defeat at Gallipoli* (see Further Reading for full details) we learn that retreating soldiers used a 'billican' device to make it seem that there were more of them than there actually were. This entailed peppering a can of water with holes so that it gradually leaked, then by fixing it to a trigger, gunfire went off intermittently over a period.

Data such as this give you a 'feel' for the real life of infantry, as does the wide reference in the poetry to army slang and nicknames. Biographies perhaps keep the reader more at a distance, being more concerned with the details of a personal experience. Both have their place, so summaries of both, wherever you find them, are useful. Most anthologies only have limited notes, so a certain amount of additional reading is needed.

Tutorial

Practice questions

1. In what ways should the critic be careful when using historical data in essays?

2. Define ideology and explain how it is visible in war poetry.

3. Why are first drafts of poems particularly useful to the critic?

Points for discussion

1. Are there any reservations a critic should have when using biographical facts to explain poems?

2. What is particularly interesting about innovative poetry in the context of a 'canon'?

Practical assignments

1. Do some research on the expressions of ideology available in German advertising and recruitment imagery or propaganda. Is this of any help in understanding how the Germans are depicted in the British war poems?

2. Read a critical essay on one of the major poets and make notes. When you have finished, try to express the critic's argument in a few sentences and try to explain how he or she has used quotation.

Study tips

1. Dip into anthologies of poetry from the Second World War and try to express the differences between the writing from both world wars in your notes. This exercise will pinpoint just how limited the geographical demarcation of the conflict was, and how such factors dictated the nature of the writing written in that context.

2. Remember to question the accepted readings of the major poets, and to be sure that you are genuinely thinking about issues for yourself on the evidence of the words in the text. The examiner wants this above all else.

10

Your Resources

One-minute summary – Largely because this subject is so vast, and also so distant, this final chapter takes you through the various support systems available to you, and the nature of self-help and organisation in studying a literary topic. There is also a need to end with a summing-up of some of the most notable aspects of this unique writing. There is an immense amount of information on the Great War in print, on the Internet and on film; so it is also necessary to provide a selection process for you, and help with the often daunting problem of knowing what is useful from this mass of materials. In this chapter you will learn:

▶ how to organise your time for study
▶ how to use the best materials
▶ what the determining features of the cultural imagery are about
▶ how best to access further information.

Setting out a reading programme

When you study an anthology in any literary area or period, there is always the problem of how to read it. This seems ridiculous, but think about it: an anthology is a large grouping of disparate and assorted writers and texts around a common theme. This means that there has been an organising principle behind the book, and generally you have to read the book following that organisation. But spend some time to think about the demands made upon you as a reader of this:

▶ *The diversity problem:* Too much historical reference, too many different writing styles, too much unfamiliar vocabulary, etc.

▶ *The time perspective problem:* The reading involves too much use of footnotes for explanation, too much stopping and starting – all caused by the nature of words and images written so long ago, when the English language was so different.

▶ *The organisational problem:* How does a person read such a book – page after page, shifting from topic to topic? Or with a plan, looking for certain things?

Why a programme?
With so much to take in, it is easy to be overloaded. Research has shown that short but intensive periods of study are better and more efficient than longer periods, in which concentration waivers and often nothing is actually learned and remembered. The following is a typical programme of study with a typical poetry anthology.

Weekly study session: one hour.
1. Choose a particular topic, e.g. friendship and relationships in war. Main primary texts (the poems themselves) – Sassoon's *To My Brother*; Alan Seeger's *The Aisne* and Owen's *Strange Meeting*.

2. Supporting reading: find an extract from Sassoon's war diary where he writes about his close friends.

3. Wider reference: read about the Pals Regiments. These were regiments recruited in a particular area in which men from the same streets and jobs would enlist together. For instance, the Leeds Pals might be part of the King's Own Yorkshire Light Infantry. There were sound tactical reasons for the military leadership to encourage this.

Using secondary texts

In the last chapter, we discussed secondary critical texts, but what about the massive amount of other related reading you might find on the shelves? For instance, a random search along the shelf in my local library gives us these categories:

▶ A nurse's memoir of work in the battlefield.
▶ A military history of the Somme.
▶ An illustrated guide to the uniforms of the infantry.
▶ A biography of a fighter pilot.
▶ A diary of an unknown soldier.

How do you select and reject when faced with this? The best answer is – don't even try! Instead, rely on only that body of knowledge that exists in the wider reference of the poetry. If you think about it, the areas of knowledge needed in reading a particular poem are quite limited, and usually in this order:

Physical world – period language – the ideology – military considerations.

Therefore, do not be tempted into reading too widely and randomly simply to feel more confident about knowing the nature of a battlefield or what a field gun looked like.

After a while, you will begin to see fairly quickly which reference or background books are to be dipped into and which should be used with more sense of purpose. For instance, a book giving you a description in words of what a 'Tommy' would have looked like is not so powerful an image as a visual sketch. Generally, illustrations will help you arrive at a clear idea of the truth and of physical detail quicker than long descriptions.

Adding other sources

There are some other sources of knowledge about the Great War, and these are often overlooked. One of these is the oral history archive. In war poetry of this conflict, what a reader needs is a direct and authentic account to compare with the poems themselves, and we are fortunate in that there are ample stocks of recorded interviews available with people who were there and who have attempted to describe their experiences. These are arguably the most useful source of information for you, and will provide insights into the psychology of the combat. There is also anecdotal memory. For instance, as a boy, I heard my grand-father talk about going 'over the top' and seeing the man running in front of him 'cop a bullet'. The man ran on for several paces, in spite of the shot, and my grandfather survived.

Oral history and local history

In a good library you will find various sources which will give a vivid account of the experience of war. For instance, the Oral History Society collects and preserves interviews with people from all trades and professions. Their collections of interviews and accounts of individual experience are always useful. Oral history provides the actual language (slang, jargon, technical terms) in use at the time, and as found in the poems. It also gives (most often) a mix of emotional and objective accounts, as in the poems themselves.

Your local newspaper can probably also provide relevant information. In 2000 for example, the *Lincolnshire Echo* published a special feature on the servicemen from the county who had won the Victoria Cross. Charles Richard Sharpe was leading a party forward to capture part of a German trench. He cleared an area of 50 yards, working alone.

There is also the newspaper archive that is well worth using. Letters to newspapers during the war also provide a fascinating insight into attitudes. For instance, the *Morning Post* carried a 'Little Mother's Letter – A Message to the Pacifists' in 1916, with these sentiments:

> To the man who pathetically calls himself a 'common soldier', may I say that we women, who demand to be heard, will tolerate no such cry as 'Peace! Peace!' The corn that will wave over land watered by the blood of our brave lads will testify to the future that their blood was not spilt in vain.

Notice how this explains perfectly the attitudes in Owen's poem *The Send Off* for example.

Summing up writing about the war poets

If we now attempt to bring all this together, and summarise the salient features of what is being asked of you in questions about this poetry, then we can say that these are the areas of knowledge you need to be competent in:

► The special nature of the poetic subject.
► The traditions dominating the conceptions of poetry at the time.
► The contrast between acceptance and questioning.
► Aspects of context: military and biographical.

It is clear from this list that a successful essay works by creating a fusion of these elements:

1. Establishing the key words and concepts in the question.

2. Qualifying these words.

3. Using a range of contrasting references to support an argument.

4. Keeping to one clear line of thought.

5. Concluding with a review of the argument.

On top of this, a good essay on the war poets introduces some relevant historical knowledge, shows a sense of context and discriminates between styles and approaches of different poets.

A survey of helpful information sources

This is an ideal point at which to survey the various sources before you read the resource section. These are the main categories open to you. Explore them all and select what is relevant.

Primary texts
These are the standard anthologies, annotated editions of the major poets, and study guides. There tend to be three types:

1. *The anthology without notes* – not really of any use to you, except that it may introduce new, lesser-known writers.

2. *The anthology with notes* – one of the very best is the type of book that explains contemporary slang and historical concepts. An example would be David Roberts' exemplary and highly recommended book, *Out in the Dark* (see Further Reading).

3. *The edition of a single poet* – in addition to your set anthology, using an edition of Owen and Sassoon is recommended. These provide explanations of words, footnotes and early drafts, showing corrections made later.

The 'feel' for the period
A useful study tip is to list the two or three general themes which interest you the most, then cluster your additional notes around the key poems. In this category are the handbooks focused on one aspect of the war such as infantry warfare or the nature of the trenches.

Literary background
A helpful type of supporting text is a reference book on twentieth century writing; this will tend to give succinct accounts of concepts and terms such as 'Georgian' and 'Jingoism'.

The Internet
There is a stunning amount of information of all kinds. The Net tends to produce real specialists, such as a researcher with a special interest in battle sites or, as in one instance, a study of literary ambulance drivers. So, the technique is to sift and sample, selecting and rejecting. The sites I list in the resources section are the result of my own sifting process.

Videos
The twentieth century wars have provided video-producers with an ongoing and reliable market. You will find a range of films about the First World War in your local library. Obviously, the value of documentary footage and pictorial images cannot be overestimated when, as a critic, you are asked to study writing from a period of a century ago. Films on this subject range from

the Royal Flying Corps to the dour imagery of attrition in the trenches.

Fiction
Why not enhance your reading with a look at fictional accounts of the war? Recent notable examples are books by Susan Hill and Pat Barker (see Further Reading). John Silkin's anthology of prose from the war is also full of fictional accounts battle.

Tutorial

Practice questions
1. What factors determine a reading programme?
2. How can you access oral materials and secondary study sources?

Discussion points
In what ways is an oral account of war comparable to a poetic account?

Practical assignments
1. Find a local newspaper of the 1914–18 period and trace letters and features that highlight the current ideology regarding Germany and the ideas of sacrifice and heroism.

2. Compare the rhetorical language of the early war poetry with that of the local newspaper features and editorials.

Study tips
1. As an exercise in study technique, read a few pages of autobiography or biography and highlight any details that seem to support your images of the war in the poems.

2. Find visual images of the 'Tommy' as in books or films about the soldier's equipment and uniform. How does an understanding of this illuminate the poems? For instance, 'trench foot' was a terrible affliction, hospitalising a huge number of combatants. Knowing about the soldier's footwear helps in understanding this, and that helps in a reading of, say, *Dulce Et Decorum Est.*

Glossary

These are the terms and concepts mentioned in the book. Chapters in which they occur are also given.

alliteration The use of clusters of similar sounds for descriptive effects (Chapter 8).

anapaestic In metre, the term given to the syllable stress pattern – – / (Chapter 6).

cadence The intonation or distinctive speech pattern in a poetic utterance (Chapter 7).

catachresis Writing in which the logic of the thought is broken or twisted for imaginative effect (Chapter 5).

catharsis The idea of 'cleansing'. That is, the view that terrible, shocking experience in art somehow releases tensions in the reader or audience or in the poet/writer (Chapter 1).

closure The type of conclusive device used to complete a poem's structure (Chapter 2).

conceit A complex variety of metaphor in which the parallel imaginative reference is hard to define (Chapter 1).

contextual Concerned with the knowledge behind and within a text, such as biography or history (Chapter 9).

dactylic In metre, the term used for the stress pattern /– – (Chapter 6).

diction The term used to describe the selected vocabulary of a poem (Chapter 1).

eclogue A classical poem involving a dialogue between male and female characters, but applied loosely to conversation poems (Chapter 7).

empathy The emotional attempt to perceive the experience of another person (Chapter 1).

Georgian The term used for the period roughly 1900–1920, referring to rural and direct, often simply realistic verse. Connected with Edward Marsh and his Georgian poetry collections (Chapter 7).

hyperbole Exaggerated statements, usually for a potent effect or humour (Chapter 1).

iambic In metre, the term used for the stress pattern – / in a foot (Chapters 6 and 8).

ideology A system of beliefs observable behind the thinking of a text (Chapters 9 and 10).

intertextuality Reference by one text to another (Chapter 2).

irony The use of a surface meaning to imply commentary on a meaning at a deeper level in a text (Chapters 5 and 6).

juxtaposition Placing side by side for effect – e.g. contrasting words or ideas (Chapter 6).

metaphor A figurative way of expression. For example: he was a very old man = a literal statement; he was as old as the hills = a metaphorical statement (mostly Chapter 4).

metre The patterns of stressed and unstressed syllabic feet in a line of verse. See **iambic**, **trochaic**, **anapaestic** and **dactylic** (Chapters 6 and 8).

octet A verse unit of eight lines, often part of a sonnet (Chapter 5).

onomatopoeia The use of words to reflect the actual sound referred to in a poem, as 'caw', 'neigh', etc. (Chapter 5).

paradox A statement that seems to make contradictory thinking (Chapter 7).

pararhyme A rhyming of the final stressed vowel, with the same sounds used after the vowel (Chapter 3).

pastoral A poem concerned with rural themes, usually idyllic (Chapter 7).

personification The metaphor variety that makes an inanimate thing behave like a sentient being (Chapter 1).

quatrain A stanza of four lines (Chapter 6).

realism The attempt to show the actual subject or experience as a reflection of the perceived reality before the poet (Chapter 1).

rhyme scheme The pattern of end rhymes at the end of lines (Chapter 2).

satire The kind of writing that attacks or ridicules wrongs, folly and error (Chapters 1 and 6).

sestet A group of six lines (Chapter 6).

simile A variety of image in which something is compared to another with the use of *as* or *like* (Chapter 5).

sonnet   A poem of 14 lines, composed of various versions of quatrains, rhyme schemes, octet and sestet (Chapter 5).

stanza   The term used for a section of a poem, separated typographically (Chapter 6).

subjectivity The appreciation or comment on something from a purely individual standpoint (Chapter 1). The opposite of objectivity, where the writer is more distant from the theme or emotion.

surreal   A technique for making the poetic subject distorted and imagistic in a way that ignores descriptive reality (Chapter 7).

symbol A type of image in which one central concept or object represents a whole set of thoughts or values around an idea (Chapter 4).

trochaic   In metre, the term used for the stress pattern / – in a metrical foot (Chapters 6 and 8).

villanelle A poem with the pattern of end-rhymes thus: ABA ABA ABA ABA ABA ABAB or variations of this (Chapter 7).

Further Reading and Reference

These titles are organised as a guide to reading rather than a general bibliography. This is to help you to select and look for items most relevant to your set text and poets.

Individual poets

Rupert Hart-Davis (ed.), *Siegfried Sassoon: The War Poems* (London: Faber, 1983)

Ian Parsons, *Collected Works of Isaac Rosenberg* (London: Chatto and Windus, 1984)

Jon Stallworthy (ed.), *The Poems of Wilfred Owen* (London: Chatto, and Windus, 1990)

George Walter (ed.), *Ivor Gurney* (London: Dent, 1996)

David. Wright (ed.), *Edward Thomas, Selected Poems and Prose* (London: Penguin, 1981)

Anthologies

E. L. Black, *1914–18 in Poetry* (London: Hodder and Stoughton, 1980)

Robert Giddings, *The War Poets* (London: Bloomsbury, 1988)

Catherine W. Reilly, *Scars Upon My Heart* (London: Virago, 1987)

David Roberts, *Out in the Dark* (Burgess Hill: Saxon, 1988). This is an outstanding book, combining texts with notes and historical contexts in a very readable form.

Jon Silkin, *The Penguin Book of First World War Poetry* (London: Penguin, 1979). Probably the definitive anthology with an extensive and detailed introduction.

Secondary criticism

Peter Childs, *The Twentieth Century in Poetry* (London: Routledge, 1999). Chapter 2 provides an excellent summary of issues about the war poetry.
Simon Fuller, *The Poetry of War* (London: Longman, 1990)
Dominic Hibberd, *Wilfred Owen: The Last Year* (London: Constable, 1992)
Dominic Hibberd (ed.), *Poetry of the First World War: A Selection of Critical Essays* (London: Macmillan, 1981)
Helen McPhail, *Wilfred Owen: Poet and Soldier* (London: Gliddon, 1993)
Hana Sambrook, *Poetry of the First World War* (London: Longman, 1997)

Biography

Keith Clark, *The Muse Colony: Dymock 1914* (Bristol: Redcliffe, 1992)
Joseph Cohen, *Journey to the Trenches: A Life of Isaac Rosenberg* (London: Robson, 1975)
Christopher Hassall, *Rupert Brooke* (London: Faber, 1964)
Jean Moorcroft, *Isaac Rosenberg: Poet and Painter* (London: Woolf, 1975)
John Stuart Roberts, *Siegfried Sassoon* (London: Richard Cohen, 1999)
Jon Stallworthy, *Wilfred Owen: A Biography* (London: Chatto and Windus, 1974)

Some historical works and memoirs

M. S. Anderson, *The Ascendancy of Europe 1815–1914* (Harlow: Pearson, 1972). This has an excellent chapter on the rise of military states and armaments.
Edmund Blunden, *Undertones of War* (London: Cobden-Sanderson, 1929)
Vera Brittain, *Testament of Youth* (London: Virago, 1978)

Robert Graves, *Goodbye to All That* (London: Penguin, 1975)

Tim Coates, *Defeat at Gallipoli* (HMSO: 2001)

A. J. P. Taylor *The First World War*. An illustrated history (London: Penguin, 1963)

Martin Gilbert, *First World War* (Weidenfeld Nicholson: 1994)

Other sources

Videos

The Great War (Castle, 1999) CHV 2010

Life in the Trenches (Castle 1999) PEG 1188

Fiction

Pat Barker's acclaimed trilogy is an interesting way to absorb the background. These are:

Regeneration (London: Viking, 1991)

The Eye of the Door (London: Viking, 1993)

The Ghost Road (London: Viking, 1995)

For a German view, the classic novel, *All Quiet on the Western Front* by Erich Maria Remarque (London: Picador, 1990) is very useful.

Pictorial etc.

Lyn Macdonald's, *1914–18 Voices and Images of the Great War* (London: Michael Joseph, 1988) is interesting.

Maurice Rickards and Michael Moody, *The First World War* (London: Jupiter, 1975). This has a fascinating range of ephemera, mementoes and documents relating to both British and German contexts.

Useful Addresses and Web Sites

General
http://www.Pbs.org/greatwar
htp://users.Tibus.com/the-great-war/
www.historytoday.com
www.ukans.edu/-kansite/ww-one/. This has documents and official
   papers, and large numbers of photographs.
www.thehistorychannel.co.uk

Poetry
The most thorough is www.hcu.ox.ac.uk/jtap/ This has features on
   specific poets and themes such as manuscript study and women
   poets.

Military context
www.worldwar1.com/
www.spartacus.schoolnet.co.uk/
www.iwm.org.uk/ This is the Imperial War Museum site.
Learn.co.uk/versailles/contents.htm

Organisations
Imperial War Museum, Lambeth Road, London SE1 6HZ
The Poetry Society, 22, Betterton Street, London WC2H 9BU
The Poetry Library, Royal Festival Hall, Level 5, London SE1 8XX
The Wilfred Owen Association, 17, Belmont, Shrewsbury, Shropshire,
   SY1 ITE

Social history
www.cfanet.com/mlewis/dict.htm
www.bbc.co.uk/history/war/wwone/1914.shtml This has contemporary newspapers.

Index